Contemporary Witchcraft

Foundational Practices for a Magical Life

Contemporary Witchcraft

Foundational Practices for a Magical Life

Frances Billinghurst

MOON BOOKS

Winchester, UK
Washington, USA

JOHN HUNT PUBLISHING

First published by Moon Books, 2021
Moon Books is an imprint of John Hunt Publishing Ltd., No. 3 East Street, Alresford
Hampshire SO24 9EE, UK
office@jhpbooks.net
www.johnhuntpublishing.com
www.moon-books.net

For distributor details and how to order please visit the 'Ordering' section on our website.

ISBN: 978 1 78904 664 9
978 1 78904 665 6 (ebook)
Library of Congress Control Number: 2020938254

A CIP catalogue record for this book is available from the British Library.

Design: Stuart Davies

UK: Printed and bound by CPI Group (UK) Ltd, Croydon, CR0 4YY
Printed in North America by CPI GPS partners

We operate a distinctive and ethical publishing philosophy in
all areas of our business, from our global network of authors to
production and worldwide distribution.

Contents

Acknowledgements   viii

Introduction   1

Part I – Background   **5**

A Brief History of Modern Witchcraft   7

What is Contemporary Witchcraft?   16

Understanding Contemporary Witchcraft   27

Common Beliefs found within Contemporary Witchcraft   34

The Wiccan Rede and the Rede of the Wiccae   49

One's Highest Ideals   58

Is Contemporary Witchcraft the right path for me?   63

Understanding and Working with Deity   72

Differences between the Hemispheres   84

The Seasonal Wheel of the Year   89

Part II – Practical   **99**

The Importance of Journaling   101

Meditation and Visualisation   104

    Exercise: Four-Fold Breath   107

    Exercise: Body Awareness   109

    Exercise: Enhancing Your Visualisation Abilities   112

    Exercise: Kim's Game   113

    Exercise: Strengthening Your Visualisations   114

The Magical Power of a Witch   116

    Exercise: Awakening the Energy   124

    Exercise: Sensing the Energy   125

    Exercise: Grounding Yourself and the Energy   126

    Exercise: Candle Visualisation   126

The Magical Circle   128

    Exercise: Casting Your Circle   133

Exercise: Breathing in Cosmic Energy   134
Exercise: Elemental Placements   139
Exercise: Creating Your Sanctuary   143
The Elements and the Elementals   145
Exercise: Air Elemental Pore Breathing   146
Exercise: Fire Elemental Pore Breathing   148
Exercise: Water Elemental Pore Breathing   150
Exercise: Earth Elemental Pore Breathing   151
Magical Working Tools   154
What is Ritual?   165
Exercise: Undertaking Your First Ritual   173
Exercise: Creating an Astral Temple   175
Four Powers of the Sphinx   177
Working with the Moon   182
Exercise: Moon Names   189
Using Herbs, Incenses and Colour   190
Exercise: Making a Gris-Gris Bag   192
The Art of Psychic Defence   197
Exercise: The Tower of Light   199
Insights into Spellcrafting   201
Living a Magical Life   211

Appendix   **213**
Basic Circle Casting Ritual   215
Elemental Pentagrams   222
Self-Blessing/Dedication Ritual   224
Cleansing Salt Scrub and Ritual Oil   228
Releasing the Power of the Witch Rite   230
Making Your Own Robe   231
Glossary   233
About the Author   239
Endnotes   241
Bibliography   246
Index   250

Acknowledgements

To my initial teachers whose wisdom inspired and encouraged me to push the boundaries.

To the elders of my tradition whose own dedication formed a source of encouragement.

To my students, past and present, whose continual queries have taught me so much.

To my Gods
who continue to reveal the Mysteries during times when it is needed the most and their words of wisdom.

Introduction

It was in the early 1990s when I took my first steps into the world of contemporary witchcraft (then generally referred to as Wicca). Back then the neophyte (beginner) was expected to learn how to render the "veils" between this world and the mystical one by applying themselves to the work in order to understand these mysteries. My initial instruction not only focused on the practical application of ritual and magick, but also the "behind the scenes" information, providing an insight into the psychological changes, as well as what is actually happening on the astral level. It is this understanding that enabled me to gain a stronger belief in the magical work that I was undertaking – a belief that also proved to be most beneficial during dark nights of the soul, the times of doubt when the logical mind saw me questioning what I had been dedicating much of my adult life to.

Processes were taught in a rather methodical manner and one's own personal practice was regularly recorded. Patience and dedication were essential requirements for the veils to be drawn back, enabling the neophyte to step through. Much appears to have changed since then.

These days Wicca has almost become a generalised term for neo-paganism, which often includes an assortment of New Age practices, as opposed to focusing on the initiatory teachings that stem from the original vision that its founder, Gerald Gardner, and later, Alex Sanders, had. Despite what seems to be a copious amount of information available today, much tends to be the same material regurgitated without any real instruction as to why or even how certain techniques are done, let alone any form of acknowledgment as to where the information was originally obtained. There also seems to be an increasing belief of "anything goes" and "do what you feel", resulting very much in a self-styled form of witchcraft with an emphasis on using one's own intuition, as opposed to foundational work.

Watching these changes occur, it seems that what is often depicted today as "Wicca" bears little resemblance to what I was trained in and what my practice involves today. While there are traditional "Wiccans" who continue to classify themselves as such, the term I personally prefer to use to describe what I do is "contemporary witchcraft".

To some this statement in itself may be controversial, after all, no one movement or person actually owns the word "Wicca" or indeed "witch" and subsequently "witchcraft". I feel, however, that coming from a more traditional background that honours oath-bound information, hierarchical training and the initiatory process, there needs to be an attempt to ensure that even a small part of what is being depicted as contemporary witchcraft (Wicca) reflects its original essence, and that the neophyte is aware of this to enable them to more accurately select their chosen path. This way some of the time-proven and time-honoured ways are retained. Therefore, throughout this book whenever you read "contemporary witchcraft" I am referring to a more traditional and initiatory form of Wicca. Where I refer to "Wicca", I am referring to the modern non-initiatory form of Wicca more commonly talked about today (unless of course I state otherwise).

Times may have changed, as have the needs and desires of people, and whilst spiritual practices also have changed, this does not necessarily mean that all of the original vision Gardner had is outdated and needs to be discarded. As the saying goes, we do not have to "throw the baby out with the bathwater". When it comes to magick, there are still aspects and techniques that simply can only be learnt over time through the practice of the magical art. Such things cannot really be taught through the pages of a book or the internet. There are other aspects of magick that are best taught under physical instruction of a trained practitioner as opposed to a handful of inexperienced novices boasting about their alleged successes.

The title of this book, *Contemporary Witchcraft: Foundational Practices for a Magical Life*, is no accident. When I teach, I like to provide students with a foundation upon which they can build their craft. This is what I feel is missing in a lot of modern books that seem to go straight to spells. While you do not need to cast a circle and honour the Gods in order to create spells and perform magick, if you wish to embrace contemporary witchcraft as your spiritual path though, then these practices are important.

Once this foundation and initial understanding of what contemporary witchcraft is actually about, then the student is able to better understand other practices that I teach. These include ancestor and spirit workings, psychic development, as well as ceremonial magick, which will be provided in later volumes.

The purpose of this book therefore is to provide the neophyte with a solid foundation and understanding of the practices of contemporary witchcraft. This material has been drawn from my own teaching notes, as well as from essays that I have written over the last 20 odd years. I further hope that the material contained within these pages compensate the lack of readily available resources for those of us living south of the equator; although Northern Hemispheric readers are also well catered for. The result is what I consider to be a rather comprehensive introduction into the foundations of the philosophies found within contemporary witchcraft.

The first section of this book contains nine somewhat detailed essays that focus on the more foundational philosophies and background with respect to contemporary witchcraft. Some of the information contained within these essays may appear somewhat controversial. This is largely due to the amount of misinformation about contemporary witchcraft that is available today.

In the second section, I have gathered together a number of

further essays that focus on the more practical aspects of the Craft, together with various exercises to assist the neophyte to gain skills that will benefit them as they walk this path. The purpose of these exercises are to enable the neophyte to begin putting into practice what they are learning.

In the final section, the Appendix, I have included an assortment of additional information that can act as a reference guide to information contained within some of the essays, as well as insights as to how to incorporate these philosophies and practices into the everyday life. Hence the title, *Contemporary Witchcraft: Foundational Practices for a Magical Life*.

Blessings, Frances
(Lughnasadh, 2020)

Part I

Background

A Brief History of Modern Witchcraft

Before diving straight into the practices of contemporary witchcraft, it is important to understand how it came about. I seem to recall that it was author and initiate of the Gardnerian tradition, Raymond Buckland, who once said that in order to know where you are going, you must first know where you have been. Archaeological evidence has revealed that spiritual beliefs appeared long before the rise of orthodox religions, including Judaism and Christianity, where there were two main images of deity: a divine male (the God), usually represented as a horned man or as a horned animal (i.e., the stag or the bull); and a divine female (the Goddess), usually represented in female form, with the emphasis placed on regenerative features. Goddess figurines date back to at least the Palaeolithic era, over 30,000 years ago, with one of the oldest being the "Venus of Willendorf" that was found in Austria. The earliest image of the Horned God appeared some 18,000 years ago in the Caverne de Trois Freres (Ariege, southern France) in the form of a cave painting that depicted a human shape (possibly a shaman) dressed in the skin of a stag and wearing antlers, dancing among bison with a hunting bow. While we will never know the true meaning of these forms of art, educated assumptions have resulted that they reflect early spiritual beliefs that may have included religio-magick (a religion or a belief system that incorporates aspects of magick). Maybe it was an early form of shamanism. What is evident is that it indicates an awakening of mankind's spirituality.

Tales of witches and witchcraft have also long appeared in classical literature, such as Greek myths that mention Medea and Circe. Both were priestesses of the Goddess Hekate, who, herself, was associated with sorcery and witchcraft, and they were also known for their magical abilities. Such stories, or at least the belief in them, became incorporated into the *Canon Episcopi* during the 12th century, a document that went on to have a profound and long-lasting impact on the philosophy that Christianity (in particular the Catholic Church, which was extremely dominant at the time) had towards witchcraft and even paganism in general.

Believed to have originally been written around 906 CE, the *Canon* considered that witchcraft was an illusion that originated in dreams and as such, to believe in it was heresy, or against the church's teachings:

> "Certain abandoned women, perverted by Satan, seduced by illusions and phantasms of demons, believe and openly profess that, in the dead of night they ride upon certain beasts with the pagan goddess Diana."[1]

In 1233, a papal bull issued by Gregory IX established a new branch of the inquisition in Toulouse, France, that was led by the Dominicans, an order of preachers founded on two purposes: preaching and the salvation of the soul. Originally the Inquisition was intended to prosecute Christian groups considered heretical, such as the Cathars. As time went by, the Dominicans eventually evolved into one of the most zealous prosecutors of persons accused of witchcraft and pagan superstition in the years leading up to the Reformation that commenced in the early 15th century. German historian Wolfgang Behringer suggests that it may have been the work of 13th century Dominican monk Thomas Aquinas that instigated this change due to his assertion that witchcraft was connected with the devil.[2]

The idea that believing in witchcraft was heresy continued until the reign of Pope Innocent VIII (1432 to 1492), who, on 5 December 1484, issued a papal bull, the *Summis desiderantes affectibus* that reversed the *Canon Episcopi* and stated that witchcraft did in fact exist and it was heresy. This bull inspired the publication of the *Malleus Maleficarum* ("The Witches' Hammer") in 1486, written by two German inquisitors of the Dominican order, Heinrich Kramer and James Sprenger, which became a handbook during the following periods of persecution known as the "witch trials" (or "Burning Times" as this period is referred to by many modern day pagan traditions).

The height of the witch trials took place between 1580 and 1630, and stretched right across Europe, resulting in the horrendous torture and deaths of many thousands of people, mostly women. The craze then continued from February 1692 until May 1693 in colonial Massachusetts, commencing in the small village of Salem. There were some 141 suspects, both men and women, tried as witches, 19 of which were executed by hanging, and one man, Giles Cory, pressed to death by heavy stones.

Despite having been distorted as the devil or evil hag or sorceress by Christianity, images of the Horned God and Goddess still remain somewhat active within the human psyche. Modern practitioners of Wicca and contemporary witchcraft continue to reject the negative Christian images, preferring to revive the more positive forms to express the ancient pagan spiritual practices.

The "birth" (or even "rebirth") of what is considered to be contemporary witchcraft occurred in the late 1930s, when a retired British civil servant and amateur anthropologist, Gerald Brosseau Gardner (1884-1964), returned to England after having spent most of his working adult life in Malay. Having an interest in spiritualism and Freemasonry, he joined a Rosicrucian theatre at Christchurch (England) in 1938, through which he met a woman by the name of Dorothy Clutterbuck (known as "Old Dot"). A year later he was initiated into a practicing coven of the "Old Religion" in the New Forest area. The practices of this coven they referred to as "Wica" (with one "c"). This introduction he recorded in *The Meaning of Witchcraft*:

"I realised that I had stumbled upon something interesting; but I was half-initiated before the word 'Wica', which they used, hit me like thunderbolt, and I knew where I was and that the Old Religion still existed. And so I found myself in the Circle, and there took the usual oath of secrecy, which bound me not to reveal certain things."[3]

In 1940, Gardner published a fictional story, *The Goddess Arrives*, which included rites closely resembling the ones from the New Forest coven. This caused controversy amongst the other coven members. His next book, *High Magic's Aid*, was published in 1949 under the pseudonym "Scire", the name he took when he was made a nominal member of infamous magician Aleister Crowley's branch of the Ordo Templi Orientis (OTO). Although fiction, this book combined natural forms of magick with high ceremony, exposing a possibility that Crowley had influenced Gardner's early work. It is said that the two met in 1946 through a gentleman by the name of Arnold Crowther, but their association was not lengthy, as Crowley died a year later. Despite this, Crowley's influence was very apparent. In particular, what is considered to be the central tenet of contemporary witchcraft, "An it harm none, do what thou wilt" is strongly suggested as patterned on Crowley's Thelemic Oath "Do what thou wilt shall be the whole of the law. Love is the Law. Love under Will". This connection is explained in more detail later when I discuss the Wiccan Rede.

It is important to remember that the British Witchcraft Act 1735 was not repealed until 1951. This meant the practicing of witchcraft up until that time was considered a crime punishable by imprisonment. Indeed, the last person to be charged under this Act was spiritual medium Helen Duncan, whose séance in 1944 was considered to be a breach of national security as she revealed the sinking of a British naval boat being sunk by the Germans that had not yet been made public knowledge.

After this Act was repealed, Gardner published two non-fiction books, *Witchcraft Today* (published in 1954) and his aforementioned *The Meaning of Witchcraft* (five years later in 1959). His reason for going public was a fear that the Craft would die out if he did not do so. These books gave details of rituals and beliefs and attracted many new initiates from the 1960s onwards.

Gardner's Freemasonry background appeared to have influenced various aspects of contemporary witchcraft including the use of three degrees of initiation, certain phrases (including "so mote it be"), the "Challenge", and initiation rite for First Degree (in part). Another influence was ceremonial magick found in the inscribing of pentagrams at the quarters, the colours and tools associated with the various elements, and the concept and use of the word "Watchtowers", which originated from Enochian (originated from medieval magician, Dr John Dee, who was also the astrologer to Queen Elizabeth I).

Gardner went public about contemporary witchcraft due to his fear that the belief system would disappear. As he was already 55 years old when he was initiated into a coven that was already filled of people older than himself, in going public he believed it would attract younger people into the Craft. He also explained that he included these other forms of magick because the rituals he received from Old Dorothy's coven were fragmentary, and in order to make them workable, he had to supplement them with material from other sources that were available to him at the time. These sources included Dr Margaret Murray's controversial work on pan-European witchcraft, *The Witch Cult in Western Europe*, *The White Goddess* by Robert Graves, American folklorist Charles Leland's *Aradia: Gospel of the Witches*, and Sir James Frazer's *The Golden Bough*, as well as various other books on ceremonial magick and the Qabalah.

From reading Gardner's books, it appears that Dr Murray's *God of the Witches* (published in 1933) as well as her earlier book, *The Witch Cult in Western Europe*, had been tremendously influential. When Gardner published *Witchcraft Today*, it contained a foreword by Murray. Despite Murray's work largely being discredited, in particular her assertion that witches were members of a secret society preserving a fertility cult that dated back to the Palaeolithic times, she still remains a source of inspiration in some circles.

It is interesting to note that many of the rituals found within contemporary witchcraft that we are familiar today were actually later additions by Doreen Valiente (one of Gardner's High Priestesses). In her own words, Valiente decided to remove a lot of Crowley and ceremonial influenced material from Gardner's Book of Shadows and substitute it with either her own writing, or that which came from more folkloristic or Celtic sources such as the *Carmina Gadelica*. As a result, Valiente is credited as having written a number of important poetic and liturgical pieces that are still immensely popular today, including the Charge of the Goddess (considered to be a paraphrase of Charles Leland's *Aradia, or the Gospel of the Witches*, first published in 1899) and the Witch's Rune.

In the 1970s, occultist Bill Liddell wrote a series of articles about George Pickingill, a "cunning man" from Canewdon, Essex in southern England. Pickingill asserted he was the progenitor of modern English witchcraft instead of Gardner. Pickingill was said to have founded some nine covens throughout southern England based on his family's hereditary practice, which was notably different from Gardner's, in that it was inundated with Norse paganism. According to Liddell, Pickingill gave his initiates a "Black Book" which included various ritual elements found within Gardner's witchcraft. This alluded to the fact that Gardner's New Forest was one of Pickingill's nine covens. Liddell also suggested the possibility that Aleister Crowley had even been initiated into one of these covens before he turned to ceremonial magick. Such claims have been disputed.

The next influential character in the evolution of contemporary witchcraft was Alex Sanders, the "King of the Witches" (as he became known after June Jones' book[4] of the same name). He was responsible for establishing what is now referred to as Alexandrian witchcraft, named after the ancient library of Alexandria, Egypt, as opposed to Sanders himself. The name was inspired by the idea that the library was an early attempt to bring together the knowledge and wisdom of the world into one place. While Alexandrian witchcraft has become one of the main traditions of initiatory witchcraft today, Sanders' life was surrounded by controversy and criticism.

Born in Manchester, England, and already a skilled healer and magician, Sanders told *Witchcraft: The Sixth Sense* author Justine Glass that he was initiated by his grandmother as a child. This initiation, however, was untrue and prior to his death in 1988, Sanders publicly apologized for his truth-bending. What remains true, however, was the fact that his grandmother, Mary Biddy, was in fact a Welsh "cunning woman", or witch.

Sanders was, however, initiated in 1963 into a Gardnerian coven by Pat Kopanski (whose magical name was "Medea"), an initiate of Patricia and Arnold Crowther (the latter had introduced Gardner to Crowley). For some reason, Sanders' entry into Gardnerian witchcraft was refused, yet he managed to obtain a copy of the Gardnerian Book of Shadows (possibly from Kopanski), to which he added his own information. Despite letters written by "Medea" (Kopanski) coming to light amongst Gardner's own personal papers to verify Sanders' initiation, there are still Gardnerians today disputing the fact.

Like Gardner before him, Sanders avidly courted publicity, which was strongly opposed by other members of the Craft, especially the Gardnerians. Some people have perceived Sanders' actions as a bid for personal notoriety; others held the view that he was profaning the mysteries. Whatever his true reason was, he attracted a strong following including Maxine Morris, some

20 years his junior, whom he married in 1967.

During the period from 1968 to 1969, Sanders and Maxine appeared in and gave technical advice on a film called "Legend of the Witches". During the press preview of the film, they met a reporter, Stewart Farrar. Stewart became interested in contemporary witchcraft, wrote *What Witches Do*, and was initiated in 1970. It was during his time in Sanders' coven that he met Janet Owen, whom he later married. The Farrars' moved to Ireland in 1976 and wrote a number of highly-respected books including *The Witches' Way, Eight Sabbats for Witches*, and *Spells and How They Work*. They worked together until Farrar's death in 2000. Janet continues to lecture on the Craft with her current partner, Gavin Bone.

Alex and Maxine separated in 1973 and Sanders moved to Sussex. He continued with his magical path until his death on 30 April 1988 (Samhain in the Northern Hemisphere), his later work being with the Ordine Della Nova (a somewhat controversial organisation that is often disputed in having any real connection with witchcraft). His funeral was said to have been a mass media event, with witches from all over England attending to pay their respects.

It is without doubt that Sanders was a controversial and flamboyant character, but despite criticism from many in the Craft, he was also both a skilled witch and a powerful magician. Like Gardner before him, Sanders brought witchcraft back into the public arena. He also changed the face of initiatory witchcraft. The Alexandrian Tradition today is said to be one of the largest traditions of the Craft, with Maxine continuing to be active.

Since the late 20th what is depicted as Wicca has largely been written about. Probably the larger influences have been the various works of the Farrars' and for solitaries, Scott Cunningham's *Wicca: A Guide for the Solitary Practitioner* in the late 1980s. My own first book on Wicca was Viviane Crowley's *Wicca: The Old Religion in the New Age*[5]. Viviane Crowley, being an Alexandrian initiate and Jungian psychologist, has probably inadvertently shaped my practice even from its initial incubation.

We can never really know the truth about the origins of contemporary witchcraft. Gardner may have been an utter fraud. He may have "invented" his own style of witchcraft, as his critics have claimed. However, to truly "invent" something would imply that his style of witchcraft had never previously existed and there is proof that Gardner did in fact draw from a pre-existing style. He may have even received a "traditional" initiation or he may have created his style of witchcraft as a result of a genuine religious experience, drawing upon his extensive literary and magical knowledge to create, or help create, the rites and philosophy. His personal library contained texts ranging beyond witchcraft that included folklore, Western philosophies, and various other magical practices.

It is important to remember that above all, as mentioned earlier, contemporary witchcraft is a "Mystery" spiritual path. Its initiates seek to understand the mystery of deity. There is no need to prove that our practices are directly descended from medieval Europe. In spirit, contemporary witchcraft is as old as time itself, and our rituals and practices should, if the belief system is to remain its relevance in the 21st century, change and adapt as humankind itself changes and adapts. One thing we can be certain of is that if there had been no more to contemporary witchcraft than an old man's fantasy, then the belief system would not have grown to be the force that it is today.

What is Contemporary Witchcraft?

The steady increase in the interest in alternative spiritual and religious practices, largely since the later part of the 20th century, has resulted in what is called "Wicca" being one of the fastest growing religions in America, Britain and Australia. According to the 2011 British census over 11,000 people identified themselves as witches or Wiccans. In America, it is estimated that 0.4% of the population (between 1 and 1.5 million people) consider themselves to be witches or Wiccans. In Australia some 6,616 people identified themselves as Wiccan, with a further 15,000 people identified themselves as being "pagan" in the 2016 census. Practitioners of contemporary witchcraft tended to fall into one or the other group.

Both Wicca and contemporary witchcraft are forms of paganism. The *Macquarie Dictionary* describes a *pagan* as an "irreligious or heathenish person", and a heathen as an "irreligious or unenlightened person". These descriptions are misleading and incorrect.

The word *pagan* originated from the Latin word *pagani* or *paganus* meaning "countryside" or "country dweller". It was a term of ridicule used by the invading Roman military for the local people, who worshipped their Gods and Goddesses in sacred groves and wild places, instead of in "proper" temples. Likewise, a *heathen* is a Nordic term meaning "one of the hearth who worships the Gods of the land". Today, the description of a "pagan" refers to various spiritual and religious practices allegedly based on, or inspired by, what we know of the ancient teachings. It should be pointed out that not all witches actually classify themselves as "pagan". Maxine Sanders, for example, readily states that she is a witch and not a pagan. I personally use the term "pagan" or "earth-centric spirituality" as generalised umbrella terms to describe what I believe in as it is easier for the general public to understand without too many preconceived ideas.

Author John Beckett[6] describes "paganism" as being organic religions that rise from the lived experiences of people in the industrial and post-industrial West that have a reverence for nature and seeing the divine in all genders. Paganism is the magick of the learned scholars as well as the magick of the ordinary folk, and it calls us to remember that good religion is a living thing, growing and changing to adapt timeless principles to where we are here and now. In his 1802 poem, "The World is Too Much With Us", William Wordsworth summed up this concept:

"The world is too much with us; late and soon,
Getting and spending, we lay waste our powers;
Little we see in Nature that is ours;
We have given our hearts away, a sordid boon!
This Sea that bares her bosom to the moon,
The winds that will be howling at all hours,
And are up-gathered now like sleeping flowers,
For this, for everything, we are out of tune;
It moves us not. –Great God! I'd rather be
A pagan suckled in a creed outworn;
So might I, standing on this pleasant lea,
Have glimpses that would make me less forlorn;
Have sight of Proteus rising from the sea;
Or hear old Triton blow his wreathèd horn."

Just as Christians or Muslins are divided into different sects, so too is paganism. There are a variety of different traditions which fall under the pagan umbrella including witchcraft (of which there are many styles), Wicca (including modern Wicca), Druidism, Qabalah (an ancient Hebrew system of esoteric philosophy), ceremonial magick, Asatru (Nordic tradition) and shamanism, as well as Western Mysticism (based the Arthurian legends), earth mysteries (ley lines), and so on. Though each of these traditions are completely separate in their teachings, most have a similar belief of honouring nature, respecting and endeavouring to understand the needs of the planet and its ecology as a whole. This, in essence, is what paganism is.

The word *occult* still conjures an element of fear in many people when, in fact, the word only means "that which is hidden". These are things which science cannot confidently explain, such as the natural energies that surround us all the time. Training in the occult arts, however, helps one get in touch with these natural energies, these hidden powers which were known to ancient man, and to bend or shape them at will. To obtain this ability, however, takes a number of years of dedication and practise, and there are some people to whom this ability will come more naturally and easily than others.

While Wicca and contemporary witchcraft may appear to be similar on the surface, there are in fact an increasing number of differences. As indicated in the introduction, contemporary witchcraft is a term I prefer to use to relate to a more traditional, and therefore initiatory practice of the Craft that can trace its influence back to Gardner, and later, Sanders. These teachings were passed down via initiation only, based on hierarchal-styled covens. At that time there were very few books available, and what there was tended to also include other teachings, some being relatively similar, that were often simply referred to as "pagan". Some of these books contained genuine practices that were considered to be oath-bound, or practices that were based on oath-bound material. When Gardner's personal Book of Shadows was made available, this led to an increased interest in initiatory-styled "Wicca" (contemporary witchcraft) that was outstripping availability of teachers and covens. Largely from the late 20th century, an explosion in published books on what was classified as "Wicca" has occurred (although often not actually originating from Gardnerian and Alexandrian trained authors). As Gardner's Wicca included the honouring of the divine feminine, a goddess, this also attracted interest from feminist and the rising Goddess or women's spirituality communities. As a result, a continuous amount of material, including a variety of interpretations, is now available to the general public and classified as "Wicca".

As mentioned previously, Gardner made no reference to "Wicca" in *High Magic's Aid* (published in 1949) with there being only three references to "Wica" in *Witchcraft Today* and some 17 references in *The Meaning of Witchcraft*. On all occasions, the word was not used to mean a religion or belief system as it is used today. Instead, Gardner referred to it as being like belonging to some exclusive club that catered only for the "wise people".

The first use of the word "Wiccan" as a person who practiced a form of magick appears to have been in 1958 by Charles and Mary Cardell (whose real names were Charles Maynard and Mary Edwards, a couple who paraded as brother and sister). The Cardells, however, spelt the word with an "e", i.e., "Wiccen". There was no love lost between the Cardells and Gardner as is evident by the following poem written by one of Gardner's friends, Margaret Bruce, about the Cardells:

"We feel it is tragick
That those who lack Magick
Should start a vendetta
With those who know betta
We who practice the Art
Have no wish to take part
Seems a pity the 'Wicca'
Don't realise this Quicca."[7]

Today, anyone seems to be able to classify themselves as "Wiccan" and it does not seem to matter if they have been initiated into a direct teaching lineage that can be traced back to Gardner or not. Whilst this is not necessarily a negative thing, as mentioned in my introduction, no one actually owns the word "Wicca", it has allowed an assortment of teachings and even ethics to now be perceived as "Wiccan" which were not originally. Additionally, this allows differing interpretations of things, including the Wiccan Rede, which may not necessarily reflect those conceptions originally held by Gardner. In fact, the word "Wicca" is often seen as being used as an alternative to "pagan", being all-encompassing as opposed to exclusive, in line with what Gardner initially envisioned.

In England, Gardnerian (the teachings extending from Gerald Gardner) and Alexandrian (the teachings of Alex Sanders) are referred to as "traditional witchcraft" (which has caused some issues with those witches who are not aligned with either Gardner or Sanders), while in the United States of America it is "British Traditional Witchcraft". Some practitioners still call themselves Wiccans, others not. As such, and due to my interest in other Craft and magical practices, I classify what I practice and teach as "contemporary witchcraft" where I attempt to keep the core element of such teachings in alignment with what has been passed down to me through the Alexandrian lineage, or at least in a similar "essence". I realise that my preference to make clear distinctions between initiatory and non-initiatory "Wicca" may appear as a form of elitism or even outdated to a seeker today. However, after nearly 30 years involvement in the Craft, I am more than comfortable with such perceptions.

Both Wicca and contemporary witchcraft tend to be belief systems that perceive deity as immanent (dwelling within) as well as transcendent (superior), and experience the divine as both masculine (the God) and feminine (the Goddess). Having said that, there are some traditions, such as Dianic Wicca, which view the divinity as purely feminine. The dual divinity that is found in contemporary witchcraft, as well as most modern Wicca traditions, can equate to the works of Carl Jung, who stated that we are all made up of a masculine (the anima) and the feminine (the animus) self. Contemporary witchcraft therefore aims to balance these energies within ourselves through the honouring and worship of the dual divinity. The Gods (a collective term referring to both the God and Goddess) within contemporary witchcraft are real – they are not archetypes, essences or even figments of one's imagination. I explain this in more depth in a later chapter.

Like the spiritual practices of Native Americans and Taoists, the spiritual practices of contemporary witchcraft intend to attune its followers to the natural rhythms and cycles of the universe as a means of personally experiencing divinity. This means that contemporary witchcraft is an "earth-centric" spiritual belief system, where rituals coincide with the various phases of the moon (full moon rituals are referred to as esbats), and the change of the seasons, solstices and equinoxes (sabbats). This ebb and flow effect is an underpinning and often overlooked aspect to contemporary witchcraft.

As mentioned previously, contemporary witchcraft is often referred to as a "Mystery" belief system. It requires the follower to undergo a ceremony (an "initiation" for a practitioner in a group or "self-dedication" for a solitary practitioner) in which certain teachings are made known to them and certain experiences undergone. Raymond Buckland once said that thMysteries of contemporary witchcraft could be shouted from the roof-top and still remain a secret, because only those people with an idea of the Mysteries would understand them. This reflected Gerald Gardner's own advice in *Witchcraft Today* where he stated that "... unless you experience it [the Craft] yourself you will never believe. When you have experienced it, you don't believe, you know."

Many practitioners of contemporary witchcraft consider their practice as a priest or priestesshood akin to the Mystery schools of classical Greece and Rome, involving years of training and passage through life-transforming initiatory rituals of different levels. I often describe the Craft as an onion, as it is through the regular practice of the rituals that the practitioner gains a deeper level of awareness or understanding of the teachings and why things are done a certain way. The latter aspect may not always be apparent at the beginning.

Both contemporary witchcraft and modern Wicca are relatively new nature-centric spiritual paths that have their immediate roots dating back to around the 1940s. Contemporary witchcraft also tends to draw inspiration from more ancient pre-Christian pagan spiritual beliefs and European shamanic practices. While a number of followers today refer to initiatory Wicca (or contemporary witchcraft) as a religion, I personally prefer to use the word "pseudo-religion" for the simple fact that the word "religion" tends to be a rather loaded word these days that has a dictionary meaning of being "the belief in and worship of a superhuman controlling power, especially a personal God or gods". The belief found within contemporary witchcraft is somewhat different.

Many contemporary witches hold the belief in higher levelled beings, i.e., Gods and Goddesses. We also perceive these aspects of the divine as omnipresent (everywhere), meaning that we are also aspects of the divine. Therefore, "worshipping" in the sense of showing reverence and adoration is the preferred used of the word within contemporary witchcraft, as opposed to the concept of "handing over" personal power and self-responsibility. This, in my opinion, makes contemporary witchcraft a "pseudo-religion" as it is not truly a "religion" when compared to more "orthodox" religions such as Christianity, Judaism and Islam.

I am fully aware that other practitioners of contemporary witchcraft may disagree with me. One person indicated that within the traditional Gardnerian and Alexandrian lineages there are specific Gods and Goddesses that are worshipped. My response is that the above explanation is purely my own, based on my own personal experience with the Gods and understanding of the word "religion"; not in any capacity of alluding that I am some form of expert on the topic. If you, the reader, consider that what you practice and how you perceive the Gods can be accurately described as a "religion", then it is.

It is becoming increasingly popular today for witchcraft to be described as solely a craft, the "craft" of the witch, void of any spiritual or religious connection. Within contemporary witchcraft there has always been this spiritual connection that indicated the Craft was more than the performing of spells. After all, in writings handed down to us from the Classical times, Medea was not only a witch but also a priestess of the Goddess Hekate, who she called upon when she traced her circles around her altar.

With the concept of deity being immanent, omnipresent and even transcendent, in his writings, magician Aleister Crowley declared that "every man and every woman is a star."[8] This suggests that we are not created in the image of God as taught by Christianity. Instead, we are "of the Gods", made from the same stuff as they are Indeed, American-Canadian theoretical physicist and cosmologist Lawrence M. Krauss has explained the scientific truth found in Crowley's statement as being:

"Every atom in your body came from a star that exploded. And, the atoms in your left hand probably came from a different star than your right hand. ... You are all stardust. You couldn't be here if stars hadn't exploded, because the elements – the carbon, nitrogen, oxygen, iron, all the things that matter for evolution and for life – weren't created at the beginning of time. They were created in the nuclear furnaces of stars, and the only way for them to get into your body is if those stars were kind enough to explode. So, forget Jesus. The stars died so that you could be here today."[9]

Within contemporary witchcraft, there is the belief that we are all of the Gods, and as such, we should conduct ourselves in such a manner, meaning we should be striving towards our highest ideals as we are advised to do by the Goddess in the Charge of the Goddess (discussed in a later chapter). This also means that within a circle, the High Priest and High Priestess are God and Goddess incarnated on this physical plane and as such, an appropriate degree of respect should be shown to them as well as humility by them.

Of course, there are stories abound of people abusing this position of power (as unfortunately are found within other spiritual and religious beliefs). However, if a person has been properly trained and undergone the degree of self-evaluation and reflection that is required during the progression of the degrees found within contemporary witchcraft, then as a High Priest or High Priestess, they should be able to act in accordance with the other moral guidelines set out in the Charge whilst running a circle, and be able to be aware when ego steps in. From personal experience, this realisation may come during hindsight, but even then, hindsight is better than total ignorance. Regardless where your practice lies within contemporary witchcraft the process of reflection and self-evaluation should be ongoing.

Contemporary witchcraft spiritual practices are intended to attune the follower with the natural rhythms and cycles of the universe as a means of personally experiencing divinity as opposed to through a third person. The rites and rituals often coincide with the phases of the moon, and the change of the seasons, as well as the solstices and equinoxes. While its practices may include the use of spell-crafting and magick, the honouring of the God and Goddess, as well as developing a greater understanding of the self, are the main focuses within both these two spiritual paths.

Origins of the Words "Witch" and "Wicca"

Many books today mention that that the word "witch" comes from *wicca* which means "to bend or shape" or "to know" and, therefore, the practice of Wicca means "the Craft of the Wise". This meaning, although poetic, is actually incorrect.

The origin of the word "witch" is an Indo-European word *weik*, which has four families of derivatives, all relating to do something with magick. The most relevant is *wikk*, which simply means "magick" or "sorcery". From this particular source, came the Middle German word *widden* which means "to predict".

From the Old English came the word *wicca* (pronounced "witcha") referring to a male witch, and the word *wicce* (pronounced "witche") referring to a female witch. From these words, came the Middle English term *witche*, and it is this word that eventually became the modern English equivalent "witch". Therefore, the original meaning of a witch, through its various forms, means simply that, a witch. It was Gerald Gardner, the founder of contemporary witchcraft, who, when writing down his ideas on witchcraft, chose to pronounce Wicca as "wikka" instead of "witcha" and from then onwards, this has been the general pronunciation.

Magic with a "K"

You may have noticed that I spell the word "magic" with a "k". The choice of spelling originated from magician Aleister Crowley who used the "k" to differentiate it from the art of stage illusion (i.e., the magic of David Copperfield and even Harry Potter). Adopting this alternative spelling also has an impact on our subconscious mind in believing in what we doing as real.

In our modern scientifically-driven world, we are continuously told that unless something can be proven (i.e., has a scientific basis) then it is not "real". Yet the realm that magick, as well as psychic abilities and even energy healing etc operate in, is very difficult to prove scientifically. While the process of changing the universe with the force of our own Will[10] maybe considered to be a mere "daydream" to the outsider, the end result to the witch, however, is very real.

Crowley only used this spelling when he referred to the word "magick" as opposed to "magical" or even "magician". As such, I have followed suit in this book.

Understanding Contemporary Witchcraft

As mentioned in the previous section, I perceive contemporary witchcraft to be a "pseudo-religious" spiritual path that calls upon its follows to engage in active participation as opposed to being merely spectators; and where each individual is ultimately responsible for the development of their own spiritual journey. Like more orthodox religions, it centres on the belief in a divine power. However, where contemporary witchcraft differs is that this divine is actually perceived as being both the masculine (the God) and feminine (the Goddess). This polarity is seen around us all the time, i.e., night and day, dark and light. It is necessary for the existence of life. As such, contemporary witchcraft can be viewed as reflecting the natural processes.

Confusion often arises due to the myriad of names used to describe the deities found within contemporary witchcraft. Depending on the personal views of the practitioner, deity may be known by those names of Gods and Goddesses that have come down to us today through ancient myths and legends. Non-initiated Wiccans may choose a pantheon based on their own heritage, or one that they feel drawn to, whether the reasons are apparent or not. Roman, Celtic, Norse, Greek and Egyptian are the more common pantheons used, but it is not unusual to find modern Wiccans honouring deities from Aztec, or even older civilisations such as Sumer and Babylonia. Within initiatory Wicca and contemporary witchcraft, however, deity is known by specific names. In fact, the knowledge of such names is usually an indication as to whether the person is a genuine initiate. This does not, however, prevent a practitioner from aligning themselves with other deities and when this occurs, the practitioner often will have various altars set aside to reflect this.

To the contemporary witch, deity is both omnipresent (meaning universal, similar to the Christian concept of deity) as well as immanent (indwelling). This thought is captured within the Charge of the Goddess, where the Goddess states:

> " ... If that which thou seekest thou findest not within thee, thou wilt never find it without thee.
> For behold, I have been with you from the beginning ..."

This statement seems to contradict a concept put forth by some people that deities, whose names are found within the pages of mythology books, are merely "archetypes", based on the partial understanding of the Jungian perception[11]. To me, this is due to a misunderstanding of the whole concept of deity, especially in the sense of contemporary witchcraft, in that I have heard it being explained that if a person "feels the presence" of deity, offers up chants or songs of praise and the like, then such actions are "too Christian". This comment, I feel, reflects a personal experience with Christianity which may not have been all that positive as opposed to the norm, as long before Christianity was even thought of, altars have been erected in the name of deity, offerings have been made, and songs of praise and hymns of devotion recorded to the Gods.

Deity is perceived as being both the divine masculine and the divine feminine. The divine masculine, the God, is generally associated with the sun and this can be echoed in other more orthodox religions. For example, within Christianity, Jesus was said to have been born around the time of the winter solstice in the Northern Hemisphere. This was the sacred time where other sun gods, such as Mithras and Attis, were also born. As the date of Jesus's birth was seen as a fixed date, when Christianity came to the Southern Hemisphere, the 25th December equated to the summer solstice, the time where the sun begins the wane in its power. If we are looking for the actual date of Jesus' birth then, when combining inferences from when shepherds would likely be in the fields and working backward from Zechariah's priestly service (John the Baptist's father), the birth date of Jesus would have more likely been somewhere from mid-September to early October.[12] Within contemporary witchcraft, the God's journey throughout life is reflected in the earth's journey around the sun and the changing of the seasons. This is explained in more depth in the "Wheel of the Year" where there are traditionally eight sabbats (seasonal observances).

The divine feminine, the Goddess, is often associated with the moon and is further known in connection with one of the three phases: the Maiden (associated with the new or waxing moon), the Mother (the full moon), and the Crone (the waxing or dark moon). The full moons (esbats) are special gatherings within contemporary witchcraft.

The cycles of the seasons are observed with special dates falling around the beginning of each season (known as the "Greater Sabbats"), as well as the mid-points of each season (the "Lesser Sabbats"). The solstices and the equinoxes, which are governed by the sun's relationship with the earth, indicate these mid-points. Coupled with these solar festivals are the monthly lunar cycles, which are important to the observance of the practitioner. As already mentioned, these are usually associated with the various aspects of the Goddess.

Unlike orthodox religions, where there is usually an intermediary (the priest) between the worshipper and the divine, the witch is in direct contact with their chosen deity. Personal altars can be easily set up within the home or outside. The most important altar, however, is always within the heart of the practitioner, as this reflects their own personal relationship with the Gods.

Another influence to contemporary witchcraft is European shamanism. In his classic book, *Shamanism: Archaic Techniques of Ecstasy*[13], historian Mircea Eliade defines a shaman as a person who enters an altered state of consciousness in order to take a spiritual journey in order to retrieve information, commune with the dead, to heal others, work magick or even to tell the future. A shaman is therefore not simply a medicine man or magician, he or she is also a mystic and psychopomp who can move between the worlds. When a witch creates a circle, they do so in order to move between the worlds, often through entering trance states, in order to commune with their Gods, to gain information, and to heal. At times, life-altering experiences or realizations are had, and new initiates undergo a symbolic death and then rebirth in order to shift the initiate's perception.

Just as modern Wicca is evolving, drawing upon new influences all the time, I believe that contemporary witchcraft is also doing the same, at least in some aspects, such as my own practice and what I subsequently teach. It is not uncommon today to find practitioners believing in what may appear to be more Eastern philosophies such as energy centres (chakras), reincarnation, and even the concept of karma. While these practices are more associated today with Eastern traditions, other ancient cultures such including Egyptian, Celtic, and Babylonian, also believed in similar concepts. Coming from a background trained in metaphysics, I also personally understand these Eastern concepts. I am mindful however that some concepts, such as karma, cannot always easily be transposed into contemporary witchcraft philosophy, especially when understood in its original concept. It is also important to note that while these differing evolutions have turned Wicca very much into a personal belief system, as opposed to a dogmatic one when comparing it to more orthodox religions, an increasing number of such evolutions has in fact taken Wicca away from its roots, the very essence or vision that Gardner had. Where you stand personally will depend on whether this is seen as a negative or positive point. I personally see the benefit of having a foot in each camp, which can be seen in what I teach and, hopefully what comes through in this book.

One thing that does stand out in the practice of contemporary witchcraft is the acceptance that we are interconnected with the world around us. We are not separate from it. This means that our actions cause a ripple effect throughout the world and even the universe, just as a stone is thrown into a pond. Taking responsibility for one's actions, be it physical, mental or emotional, is an important aspect to following both these spiritual paths. When this is properly understood on a personal level, it influences how a practitioner conducts themselves at all times.

Understanding one's place within the cyclic universe can be a very daunting process at the best of times, but it can be obtained if a person is truly dedicated to undertaking this challenge. It does involve a lot of self-work and personal discovery, and what is discovered is not always pleasant, but in order to spiritually evolve, such work is necessary. Contemporary witchcraft helps the practitioner to do just this. One guide to assist this is the axiom "as above, so below, as within, so without", which is one of the seven principles of Hermes Trismegistus, the alleged author of *Hermetic Corpus*, a series of sacred texts that are the basis of Hermeticism, itself being a religious, philosophical, and esoteric tradition that has deeply influenced Western magical thought. While there are numerous interpretations of this quote, the common one is that the "as above" refers to the cosmos, the divine, the land of the Gods, what is external to ourselves, the macrocosm; "so below" refers to us, what is inside of us, the microcosm; "as within" (our thoughts), "so without" (what is projected or attracted in the world around us). The whole universe therefore is reflected in each person and as such each person also reflects the universe. In other words, when we understand ourselves, we understand the universe.

When this axiom is applied to contemporary witchcraft and magick, it can be interpreted as this: the circle that we cast in order to contain the energy that we raise is our own world, the microcosm. The universe, or the realm of the Gods that we project this energy out into is the macrocosm.

Many spiritual and religious belief systems have their own methods to assist the seeker in doing self-work. Contemporary witchcraft is no different. Insight can be given through many forms, such as meditation, divination, psychic impressions, or even dreams. Revelations, the "ah-ha" moment, can occur out of the blue, or subtle signs may be given to those who are more observant. I have personally had instances where the sign I have asked for has come in some form as simple as a feather, or as life-changing as being made redundant, or even the diagnosis of an illness. It is how we react and interpret these signs which is one of the mysteries of many spiritual belief systems. Such knowledge is not found in books but through personal observances, contemplation and experience.

There are no scapegoats within contemporary witchcraft, no adversary to blame when things do not go according to our perception of how it should. We attract all those instances, the pleasant and the not so pleasant, into our life in order to learn the lessons we need to learn, in order to evolve more spiritually and to connect us, often on a deeper level, to what is really important. Often this is a very hard lesson to learn in a society where our behaviour is largely dictated by social media and tends to focus solely on physical aspects as opposed to more spiritual ones.

As with all spiritual paths, religions and other like belief systems, contemporary witchcraft is very much about the personal connection with the divine and the bringing of this peaceful connection within, so that it encompasses all aspects of your life. If anything, contemporary witchcraft forces us to deal with our own issues – all those psychological aspects, uncertainties and fears, emotional or mental issues that we tend to either sweep under to carpet and ignore, or project onto other people. I should point out that this does not mean that the contemporary witchcraft "fixes" these aspects, nor is it a one-stop-shop cure-all. If anything, the opposite happens. Contemporary witchcraft brings such issues to the surface where we are forced to deal with them, often through seeking professional help, engaging in the hard work and making the hard decisions once and for all.

Contemporary witchcraft tends to be a tradition of the Craft that includes the process of initiation. Initiation rites had originated from our earliest hunter and gatherer communities where they marked specific times in a person's life. These rites usually required the person undergoing some kind of pain or challenge – such as a vision quest, circumcision, scarification, or even bloodletting. Therefore, the ordeal was not something that was entered into lightly.

Common Beliefs found within Contemporary Witchcraft

Having given a somewhat basic overview of what contemporary witchcraft is about, it is now time to move down to a deeper layer of the proverbial onion and look at some of the more common beliefs. On the surface it is safe to say that contemporary witchcraft has very little, if any, associated dogma (i.e., a doctrine or system of doctrines proclaimed by authority as true). Many practices are derived from within, are often personal to the individual and are not mandated by any one person, hierarchy, or "bible". It is not uncommon for people who have been brought up in a more organised orthodox religion not used to such open and free belief systems to find this challenging initially. It does takes time to become comfortable in developing your spiritual practices from personal experiences and knowledge, but therein lies the beauty of earth-centric paths such as contemporary witchcraft.

The lack of doctrines, however, does not mean a lack of ethics. Many practitioners of contemporary witchcraft follow a number of ethical codes that are somewhat similar to the essence of those which can be found within other spiritual and religious beliefs, including what is referred to as "The Golden Rule". (This originated with Pittacus, one of the seven ancient sages of Greece, who in 650 BCE stated: "Do not to your neighbour what you would take ill from him". Today we are more familiar with the Christianised version of "Do unto others as you would have them do unto you"). Within contemporary witchcraft, there can be found three main ethics, or variants of them, two of which are often misinterpreted and therefore misunderstood.

The Wiccan Rede

What is commonly referred to as the Wiccan Rede is in fact the last two lines of a longer poem known as the Rede of the Wiccae:

"Eight words the Wiccan Rede fulfil:
An it harm none, do what ye will."

The Rede of the Wiccae itself is a 26-lined poem that first appeared in 1975 in an American pagan magazine, *The Green Egg*. This poem had been provided by Gwen Thompson (1928-1986), the founder of the New England Covens of Traditionalist Witches (NECTW), and was allegedly passed down to her by her grandmother, Adriana Porter. Thompson indicated that the purpose for sharing this poem was to provide accurate information with respect to the Wiccan and contemporary witchcraft practices, some of which can be found within the poem.

There is a somewhat interesting fact about the Rede of the Wiccae and in particular the last two lines, the commonly referred to Wiccan Rede, and that is that this phrase was first published in a British newsletter, *The Pentagram*, in 1964, where it was attributed to a speech made by Doreen Valiente on 3 October 1964 at what may have been the first witches' dinner organised in modern history. In the speech she referred to an Anglo-Saxon witch formula known as the Wiccan Rede, or wise teaching. This article, or at least this part of Valiente's speech, was subsequently reprinted in an American newsletter, *The Waning Moon*, in 1966, to which Thompson was believed to have subscribed. While I am not intending to cast any aspersions upon Thompson, I do find the crossover rather interesting.

One of the somewhat confusing things about contemporary witchcraft is the various interpretations, stories, and essential mythos that make up the Craft history today. I consider these add to the richness and mystique at the end of the day. Whilst it is important to have a basic understanding of history, I advise my students not to get too caught up in the personalities. Rather, I advise them to focus on the contributions of the individuals.

The possible source of these eight words, "An it harm none,

do what ye will", is believed by some people[14] to be the Thelemic Oath of Aleister Crowley, and may have been one of Crowley's writings that Valiente removed from Gardner's original Book of Shadows. The Rede, when quoted in full, states:

"Do as thou wilt shall be the whole of the Law.
Love is the Law, Love under Will."

The first part of the Thelemic Oath, *"Do what thou wilt shall be the whole of the law"*, means that it is the obligation of each of us to do as our True Will, or higher self, directs, as this leads to spiritual fulfilment. Crowley also stated that "Every man and every woman is a star". Each of us has our own light to give to the world; each of us has our own orbit, our path through the universe, a way which is right for us and us alone. This can be further emphasised by *The Bhagavad Gita*[15] where it states, "It is better to do one's own dharma, even though imperfectly, than to do another's dharma, even though perfectly." Dharma being the Buddhist or Eastern concept of cosmic law and order. Only you can judge which action is right for you at any one time. To stop growing, to become rigid and unbending is to start dying. Chinese classic, the *Dao De Jing*, says "Rigidity and hardness is the stigmata of death; elasticity and adaptability of life."

The second part of the Thelemic Oath, *"Love is the law, love under Will"*, shows that the nature of our True Will must always be love. Love is the yearning for things which are apart to become unified. Love is how we reach out beyond ourselves to that which we desire. Although we are individual stars, we are never alone in our own ivory tower. While each of us shines with the innermost light, the universe is full of other stars, each of these shining its own radiance towards us. Love is the function of the True Will and as such should never be used as a weapon or a tool to manipulate the Will of others, nor allow others to restrict our own Will.

Regardless of its origins, the main problem with the Wiccan Rede is that it is often misquoted with people reversing its construction so that it reads: *"Do what ye will, an it harm none"*. In this reversed format, the Rede is easily interpreted as meaning do what you want as long as it harms none or nothing. Not only is this interpretation impossible to live up to, it also changes the Rede from a "guideline" (as was its original intention and what the word *rede* actually means) to a "prohibitive commandment".

Due to the somewhat complex nature of the Wiccan Rede, largely because of this misinterpretation, I will discuss it, its meaning and application, and the importance of understanding it accurately, in most depth in the following section.

The Law of Cause and Effect

Another belief found within contemporary witchcraft is the Law of Cause and Effect where "every action has an equal and opposite reaction". The Law of Cause and Effect is the axiom reminding us that nothing happens by sheer chance, as everything is inter-connected. It states that many things may seem like coincidences have a cause somewhere. The cause may not be physical in nature, but mental or magical, and that things when things occur, they do so for a reason where the root of that reason may be elsewhere. Often, the effect of one action becomes the cause of another, creating a chain of events.

Every action you take, every thought and feeling you have cause an effect, to you or to someone or even something else. If your every action has a result, you must be careful and accept responsibility for everything you do.

American writer Ed Fitch[16] advises that the Law of Cause and Effect originates in the akasha (ether) principle, and thus is not affected by time or space. This immutable law works everywhere in the most obvious, to the most extremely subtle, manner. Therefore, every deed either proceeds from a cause or is followed by a result, whether in the blinking of an eye or in two thousand years.

A misunderstanding with respect to the Law of Cause and Effect seems to be found within modern non-initiatory Wicca that it is connected to, or even an alternative to the law of karma found within Hinduism and Buddhism. According to these Eastern beliefs, we are trapped in a seemingly endless cycle of reincarnation (samsara) from which we are attempting to free ourselves from by pursuing enlightenment (samadhi). What we attract during this endless cycle of reincarnation is our karma, the result of our actions in accordance with dharma, universal law. I provide my own insights into reincarnation from a contemporary witchcraft perspective later in this chapter.

The Threefold Law of Return

Connected to the Law of Cause and Effect is the somewhat controversial and often misquoted Threefold Law of Return, where the belief is that whatever goes forth whether of good or ill, must return threefold; for our actions affect more than people generally realise, such as:

"Whatever you send forth, whether of good or of ill,
returns to you threefold."

The concept of the threefold law of return is largely considered to be a misinterpretation from *High Magic's Aid* wherein Gardner's fictional protagonist undergoes an initiation rite in which he is taught "mark well when thou receivest good, so equally art bound to return good threefold". In other words, when someone does good by a witch, it is the witch who is bound to return that good threefold, not the doer. In other words, it is considered beneficial for a person to bless, help or aid a witch, as it is the witch who is the agent of a threefold response, not the universe.

As far as I am aware, the Threefold Law of Return does not actually appear anywhere within Gardner's actual Book of

Shadows. However, the following short poem was attributed to the aforementioned Gwen Thompson and could explain why it has been incorporated into the teachings of both contemporary witchcraft and Wicca, possibly hinting to an American influence despite Thompson not actually having been initiated into Gardner's Wicca (she claimed to be a hereditary witch from an established family tradition):

"Ever mind the Rule of Three
Three times what thou givest returns to thee
This lesson well, thou must learn
Three only gets what thou dost earn!"

A modern approach to looking at the Threefold Law of Return can be that it illustrates the power underlying our intentions. Our intent determines the approach we take to life. Our actions determine the response life takes to us.

In modern Wicca, while the Wiccan Rede is considered to be an ethical statement, the Threefold Law of Return is considered to be a moral one. Our actions and words ripple outwards from us, touching other lives in one way or another. Every good deed we do, every helping hand we lend, and every time we act responsibly, we improve our society by fostering an environment in which positive actions begin to outnumber negative ones. For the follower of contemporary witchcraft this is worth considering.

While some people may take the Threefold Law of Return literally, the number three is actually symbolic:

- Once for the planting, once for the nurturing, and once for the harvest.
- Once for the thought, once for the word, and once for the deed.
- Once for the effect on our own character and karma, once

for the declaration of that act as something we ourselves are subject to, and once for its effect on the intended subject.

The Threefold Law of Return challenges us to find a constructive, yet positive, way to deal with the situations we face in the course of our lives. We all are part of the world, and our relationships with other people are still very much our own matter to deal with. We all have to live with the consequences of our actions and the fruit of our intentions. This means that witches should pay attention to the energies they send out as they should not want to negatively impact anyone, even indirectly.

Intent without action is worthless and action without intent is worse than useless – it can be harmful. The Threefold Law of Return demonstrates the importance of right intent, and reveals the secret to bringing about real prosperity. When our actions are true expressions of our intentions, our True Will, or higher self, we are doing magick.

There are two other aspects of contemporary witchcraft that I feel also belong in this section. They are:

- **The Law of Self-Responsibility**: The universal Law of Attraction states that we attract all into our lives, therefore we are ultimately responsible for what we exchange with others, including thoughts, actions, and words. Hence the Law of Self-Responsibility. When we expand upon the idea of self-responsibility, we find ourselves returning to Crowley's Thelemic Oath as mentioned earlier. Whilst not a true part of the teachings within contemporary witchcraft, considering it is from this oath that the "short version" of the Rede originates, it seems appropriate to expand on its meaning.
- **The Ethic of Attunement**: Contemporary witchcraft is primarily a spiritual belief that believes in the polarity of

deity, i.e., both masculine and feminine where, like the Taoist yin/yang, in order to create perfect harmony and balance, one aspect cannot truly exist without the other. When we attune ourselves to the divine, we in effect get in touch with that "divine" aspect within ourselves as well, in order for us to receive communication from deity. The more we perform and practice the ethic of attunement, the more in touch we become with our Higher Self. This, in turn, enables us to act in accordance with our True Will more readily, thus attuning more readily to the universe as a whole.

When awareness is embraced that everything within the universe is interconnected through the Law of Vibration, then a natural part of the spiritual evolution of contemporary witchcraft is to raise one's own level of vibration in order to "attune" oneself with the rest of the universe. There are numerous ways that this can be achieved, including through the regular practice of meditation, observation of the natural world around us, as well as through the various rites undertaken within the training of contemporary witchcraft.

Other General Beliefs

There are a number of generalized beliefs that can be found not only within contemporary witchcraft, but also within Wicca and other pagan spiritual belief practices as a whole. These include:

- **Life is Sacred**: Pagans, in general, believe all life is sacred and that includes other beings beyond human. Many witches therefore belong to environmental organisations and animal welfare groups, as well as other worthy organisations. The earth is reserved as our mother and therefore, witches are concerned about the environment and quality of life for those less fortunate than ourselves.

I personally view this belief as not one exclusive to contemporary witchcraft or paganism, but for any environmentally or consciously aware person, regardless of what spiritual or religious belief system they may have. A more contemporary witchcraft interpretation is outlined below under "Reverence for the Earth".

- **Sex is Sacred**: Sex between consenting adults is seen as a sacred gift bestowed upon humans from the Gods, and is something which should be enjoyed. Therefore, it is important to have a positive and healthy approach to sex and sexuality. This means that some of the more restrictive perceptions placed upon sex and sexuality by other faiths, and in particular attitudes towards the LGBTQ+ community, should not apply in this day and age. While I realise that some people may consider this to be at odds with the somewhat homophobic writings of Gardner, I consider it is important to keep in mind that times, and indeed society, has moved on greatly since the late 1940s and 50s. As such, the Craft should also reflect this, and indeed today many contemporary witchcraft covens teach not only to see the God in every man and the Goddess in every woman but also the opposite, i.e., the God in the woman and the Goddess in the man – as if to reflect the Jungian concept of the anima and animus.

Due to the amount of abuse that has occurred within various spiritual and religious traditions (and neither Wicca nor contemporary witchcraft are immune to this), I believe it is important to state from the outset that sex in any way, state or form is never considered to be an appropriate "payment" or "exchange" for teachings of the Craft. In fact, there are few occasions where it may be used, and even then, often within the context of a normally partnered couple (if both are witches within the circle) or between consenting adults if other magical practices are engaged (i.e., Third Degree initiation when performed in reality or sex magick). It is extremely rare, if at all, that a seeker or neophyte be exposed to such practices. Ritual nudity on the other hand is something that the seeker or neophyte may be exposed to if the coven they are seeking to join is a "sky-clad" coven. As far as I am aware, all Gardnerians practice their rituals sky-clad. The same, however, cannot be said for Alexandrian covens. If you are working skyclad in a coven, a general rule of thumb is that this should not be interpreted as an open and ongoing invitation. Consent should be asked and never assumed.

- **Dark is not Evil**: There is a natural light and dark to the universe. This polarity is a part of the natural order of things and is not necessarily evil or bad. What is considered "light" are those events or processes which are beneficial. "Dark" are things that might be harmful. Death, for example, is dark, but as it is part of the natural process of life, it is not feared by witches and other pagans alike.

Evil is different from "dark" especially when it is used to describe human actions. If a volcano erupts and destroys a village, this action is considered to be "dark" as there was no evil or malicious intent on the part of the volcano. However, if a person commits murder, this individual has set out to harm another and, therefore, their action can be described as "evil". The same can be said for any other action that is taken purely for personal gain without consideration of its flow on effect on others. Therefore, it is not only the act, but the malicious intent that differentiates "evil" from "dark".

Given the above points, contemporary witches are opposed to the abuse of any individual and of nature, including animals and birds, plants and the earth itself. This includes:

- physical abuse,
- violence and mental cruelty,
- psychological manipulation and power trips,
- sexual abuse,
- abuse through others for commercial gain,
- financial abuse by any dishonest or illegal activity,
- religious intolerance or political abuse, or
- the abuse of any living thing on earth or damaging the environment.

- **All is Positive and Negative**: For every positive there is a negative, for light there is darkness, and for the masculine, there is feminine. This is polarity, and it is impossible to have one without the other. In Eastern tradition, this is evident in the symbol of *yin* (relates to the feminine, is negative and means "dark side of the mountain") and *yang* (relates to the masculine, is positive and means "light side of the mountain"). This is part of the natural cycle of polarity mentioned above.

- **Reincarnation**: Reincarnation, the doctrine of rebirth, has been around for as long as humankind has considered the fate of one's personality, when the body has literally given up the ghost. In a nutshell, the phenomenon of repeated incarnations in human form is to allow the evolution of the ageless, sexless human soul. The process is certainly not an exclusive contemporary witchcraft concept, but it is happily embraced by most because it helps to justify birth, death and karma.

  As mentioned earlier, within contemporary witchcraft there is also the belief of life after death – that we all have lessons to learn and such lessons cannot be learnt in one lifetime. Central to the seasonal mythos that is more commonly known as the "Wheel of the Year", the God follows the natural cycle where he dies each autumn in order to be reborn (i.e., reincarnated) at the winter solstice.

Further, within The Charge of the Goddess the Goddess states:

"For I am the Soul of Nature, who giveth life to the universe;
from me all things proceed, and unto me must all things return ...".

From the outset, followers of contemporary witchcraft do not attempt to escape rebirth, or reincarnation. Instead, reincarnation is embraced, as it is one of the few tenets that is actually found within the written text, in particular the Charge of the Goddess. Therefore, the only aspect of karma that is found within contemporary witchcraft is the need of our soul to learn and/or gain experiences throughout its evolution.

• **Reverence for the Earth**: The planet, our earth, is often perceived as a manifestation of deity. The natural processes, for example, the seasons, day and night, fertility, are undetermined by human intervention. They are directed by divinity and, as such, are considered sacred. Ultimately this leads to a concern for the earth and the environment. It is not uncommon to see contemporary witches, as part of their honouring the earth, devoting time and resources to environmental issues - from personal recycling and water conservation, to being actively involved in environmental organisations. It is generally considered that the earth is our mother, Gaia (from Greek mythology), and this belief can be seen all over the world in various indigenous societies.

Contemporary witchcraft practices are earth-centric and therefore our relationship with the earth is important as it reflects the microcosm and macrocosm, as without so within, our actions as to how we live and our planet also reflect our relationship with ourselves. This follows on from the general belief that all life is sacred.

- **Use of Magick**: Magick plays a role in many religious and spiritual paths, even though it is not widely described as such. Were the "miracles" of Jesus Christ not displays of magick, when he fed the masses using a couple of fish and a few loaves of bread? Or when Moses parted the Red Sea? In today's Christian churches, the priests, in full view of their congregation, turn bread and wine into the body and blood of Christ. The only difference between this form of magick and that which is practiced within contemporary witchcraft, is that in more orthodox religions, the practice of magick is restricted to higher office bearers. In contemporary witchcraft, the rituals are available to all those seekers who are interested in learning our version of the Craft. Magick is therefore a natural part of life and as such an integral part of contemporary witchcraft.

A summary of the above can also be expressed through the 13 simple goals, or tenets, that American Wiccan author Scott Cunningham wrote about in his *Wicca: A Guide for the Solitary Practitioner*[17]. While the book itself focuses on the modern adaptation of Wicca as opposed to contemporary witchcraft, these goals give ideas as to how to incorporate the above ethics into your life:

- Know yourself.
- Know your Craft.
- Learn.
- Apply knowledge with wisdom.
- Achieve balance.
- Keep your words in good order.
- Keep your thoughts in good order.
- Celebrate life.
- Attune with the cycles of the earth.

- Breathe and eat correctly.
- Exercise the body.
- Meditate.
- Honour the divinity (Goddess and God).

Having looked at the beliefs of contemporary witchcraft, I wish to address a few common misunderstandings and falsehoods that are still lingering about the Craft.

- **It is anti-Christian**: Just because a belief system is not something else does not mean it is "anti". While this may be the case for many orthodox religions (especially Christianity and Islam) which both, ironically, actually have a lot in common, it is not the same for contemporary witchcraft. The Charge of the Goddess states that as she is the mother of living, her love is "poured out upon the earth" for all inhabitants regardless of religious or spiritual beliefs, gender, age, race or even species.

  These days there are even people who describe their practice as "Christian Wicca" or "Christian Witchcraft". These concepts I personally find difficulty to comprehend, largely due to Biblical references (using the *King James Bible* as a source) such as those found in Exodus 22:18 that "Thou shalt not suffer a witch to live" and Exodus 20:3-4 "Thou shalt have no other gods before me" and "Thou shalt not make unto thee any graven image, or any likeness of anything that is in heaven above, or that is in the earth beneath, or that is in the water under the earth."

  However, save from condemning another's practice as incorrect, while I do not feel that such beliefs fall into my own perception of Wicca and what contemporary witchcraft means to me, as indicated in the beginning, I do not "own" the word "witch" therefore each to their own.

- **Witchcraft is Satanic**: As Satan is part of the Christian belief system, it therefore has nothing to do with contemporary witchcraft. My understanding of Satan is that the word was originally used as a "job description", i.e., the Satan. When the Christian God wanted to test the strength of Job's devotion to him, it was Satan who actually did the testing.

Satan can be transposed with the word "devil" who has appeared in numerous guises through the *Bible* and other Christian writings. These guises have included a black dog, a man with a top hat, as well as the more familiar figure with cloven hooves and horns. The latter tends to be a reflection of older nature Gods – in particular, the Greek God Pan – leading to a belief that this was a method of conversion utilised by Christians to depict the Old Gods as evil.

Within one of the early "creation" myths of the Craft, reference to Lucifer can be found. In this context, he is referred to as the "light-bringer" within the Craft and was originally considered as the star of the east, prior to Christianity incorporating him into its own mythos where he fell to earth.

- **Proselytizing for Followers**: Within contemporary witchcraft, there is no need to convert seekers as people are considered free and have the right to believe or not believe in whatever they wish. Seekers are also free to make their own choices, including investigating other belief systems if they determine that contemporary witchcraft is not for them.

The Wiccan Rede and the Rede of the Wiccae

Probably the most misinterpreted and misunderstood aspect of contemporary witchcraft is the Wiccan Rede – what it means, and whether or not it applies to people who do not identify as Wiccans or have not been trained in contemporary witchcraft. Earlier, I referred to the Rede as being a guideline, as opposed to a prohibitive command. This can be simply be realised when considering that the word *rede* means "to counsel or to advise", and as such, neither it, nor the Rede of the Wiccae, had ever meant to be some form of the Ten Commandments. No one is bound to obey every statement made in the Rede in order to be a "true Wiccan" or witch.

In its true meaning as a guideline, the Rede advises the path of least harm is the ethical path, and that we should always think before we act: "An it harm none, do what ye will." We are to take responsibility for the consequences of our actions (as well as our thoughts and deeds), as well as the results of such if we fail to act. The latter is something that can be overlooked. This means that by *not* acting to prevent harm, we may also be the cause of it through by an act of omission rather than commission. To explain this another way, Irish politician and philosopher, Edmund Burke (1729 – 1797) wrote:

"All that is needed for the triumph of evil is for good men to do nothing."

This concept where doing nothing can create more harm than doing something predates Burke by over a thousand years, as Chinese philosopher Lao Tse stated:

"When the proper man does nothing (wu-wei), his thought is

felt ten thousand miles."

When it comes to who should follow the Rede, it is my view that as the Rede is clearly referred to as "Wiccan" or "Wiccae". It is somewhat preposterous to assume that all pagans should abide by it, even those people who identify themselves as "witches" but who are not aligned with Gardnerian-influenced contemporary witchcraft. The Rede is clearly a guide for those do align themselves with Gardnerian-influenced witchcraft as well as modern day Wicca, for when the "long version" of the Rede is considered, it outlines certain ritual practices, lore and other insights into the practices and beliefs of both contemporary witchcraft and Wicca. Of course, should a pagan or a witch following a non-Gardnerian-influenced path wish to observe the Rede as part of their own personal ethical code, then there is nothing preventing them from doing so. For those readers who may not have come across the Rede of the Wiccae, or the "long version", this can be provided at the end of this section at the rear of this book, together with an interpretation of what each line means.

Further confusion about the Rede tends to stem from the opening line, "Bide ye Wiccan laws ye must", with people misinterpreting this to imply that the Rede is a law that should be followed by all. The word *bide* does not mean "obey"; it means "endure". This highlights a further misconception when only parts of the Rede are considered, as opposed to the whole.

Contemporary witchcraft is a spiritual belief that assumes its followers will have enough maturity to use their powers wisely. Each witch, particularly when a certain level of initiation is attained, can decide the course of their life and make their own decisions based on their own judgement, and that these are in alignment with their "highest ideals" as we are advised in the Charge of the Goddess. (The concept of "highest ideals" is discussed in the following section.) However, self-government does not work without self-discipline. Where the Rede tends to fail is when it is applied by people who lack or lose sight of this self-discipline. Freedom is the opportunity to take responsibility for one's own actions. The Rede grants this freedom and, in turn, places the responsibility for a witch's actions entirely on the shoulders of that person. This can also be said for all practitioners of magick, regardless of what tradition they follow.

Returning to Valiente's eight-worded Rede of "An ye harm none, do what ye will", misinformed people often consider that this means "harm none" - no one or nothing, including the world around them. While this is very admirable, it is actually impossible in reality, as American Wiccan author Kaatryn MacMorgan[18] advises:

- If you breathe, you harm microbes that die upon contact with your respiratory tract.
- If you eat, you harm animals, plants, yeast, and even moulds that live in most foods.
- If you reproduce, you create a drain on the natural resources, and if you do not, you are not able to pass on your genes.
- You cannot even go into the forest and die from not breathing and eating because you will kill plants when you land upon the ground as well as from over-fertilisation when your body starts to decompose.

The Rede therefore is a philosophy of taking responsibility for our own actions all of the time. Nowhere does it actually tell us to do things that do not harm. Instead, it advises us that we should endeavour to do things that harm nothing. This leaves us to our own discretion as to the other actions with respect to any other given situation where the outcome may cause harm.

On the whole, the Rede is a life-affirming statement, meaning that its followers have to think about their actions and their effects on the self, on other people, the society as a whole and the environment, not just now but also in the future.

MacMorgan redefines the Rede as "Do as you will, if it harm naught - if it harm some, do what you ought"[19]. The "ought" is defined within the rest of the teachings found within contemporary witchcraft, including the Charge of the Goddess. This means becoming aware of your thoughts, actions and deeds so that you know your True Will, or your "highest ideal". Your True Will is your intention, your desire, and it is based on knowledge of the Self. Everyone who knows their Will can do their Will, can act within their intention, desire and knowledge of the Self to achieve an end. The difficulty is self-analysing whether we are indeed acting in accordance of our free will, or one encased with ego. Once again, we can turn to the Charge of the Goddess, which it reminds us that whenever possible, acts of humility should be undertaken.

The Rede works as a theology because it is not restrictive. When theology is spoken in terms of "dont's", it becomes a set of rules. The study of the ancient Gods and the pursuit of a relationship with them is not about *not* doing things, but actually about doing things.

The Rede has become the major underlying principle of the contemporary witchcraft belief and is so powerful a statement that it has been adopted by other pagans. How far you personally apply the Rede is up to you. However, it becomes more important when applied to magick and psychism. This is because once you have developed these skills, it becomes more possible to be able to influence people, positively or negatively, depending on your own personal moral code.

The Rede of the Wiccae

There are a number of versions of the Wiccan Rede, not to mention interpretations of it. What follows is the original "Rede of the Wiccae" that was also known as the "Counsel of the Wise

Ones" that Gwen Thompson provided to the American pagan magazine, *The Green Egg,* which she allegedly received from her grandmother, Adriana Porter.

Of the 26 lines, 12 contain metaphysical information or common British folklore and divination; ten lines relate to ritual practice that inner court coven members should know about; while of the remaining four line, two contain ritual language and two the naming of the Wiccan laws (the Ardanes). The lines in italics are a generalised interpretation.

1   Bide the Wiccan Laws ye must in Perfect Love and Perfect Trust.
    Possible reference to the Old Laws, the Ardanes, that were first revealed by Gardner to other members of his coven in 1957.

2   Live an' let live - fairly take an' fairly give.
    Preserve life; both yours and others, balance the concept of giving and receiving, and do not take advantage of others or let others take advantage of you.

3   Cast the circle thrice about to keep all evil spirits out.
    Circles are often circumnavigated three times when casted in order to form a protective barrier.

4   To bind the spell every time - let the spell be spake in rhyme.
    Spells are believed to have more power when they rhyme, or at least they are easier to recite and roll off the tongue. This does not mean to say that you cannot use spells, chants, or incantation that do not rhyme.

5   Soft of eye an' light of touch - speak little, listen much.
    When interacting with others, do so openly. Listen to what they have to say before thinking of your response or interrupting.

There is a saying that states: "You have two ears and one mouth".

6   Deosil go by the waxing moon - sing and dance the Wiccan rune.
     Deosil (with the sun) is the usual way to cast and move around a circle. When the moon is waxing, it is increasing in size. The Wiccan Rune is a chant penned by Doreen Valiente.

7   Widdershins go when the moon doth wane, an' the werewolf howls by the dread wolfsbane.
     Widdershins (against the sun) is associated with banishing. When the moon is waning, it is decreasing in size. Wolfsbane is a highly toxic plant.

8   When the Lady's moon is new, kiss thy hand to Her times two.
     Folklore states that if you send two kisses to the new moon you will have to bring good luck and prosperity as the moon increases in size.

9   When the moon rides at Her peak then your heart's desire seek.
     Referring to the time of the full moon, which is the ideal time to do spells to attract things into your life.

10   Heed the north wind's mighty gale - lock the door and drop the sail.
     In the Northern Hemisphere, the north wind represents winter, the time to lock up and settle in for the cold days season ahead.

11   When the wind comes from the south, love will kiss thee on the mouth.
     In the Northern Hemisphere, the south winds represent

summer, the time of warming after often long cold winters.

12 When the wind blows from the east, expect the new and set the feast.
East winds are often associated with new and unexpected activities, and are often associated with spring.

13 When the west wind blows o'er thee, departed spirits restless be.
The west wind is associated with autumn, the time when the earth begins its transition into hibernation. It is also the season associated with death and departure.

14 Nine woods in the cauldron go - burn them quick an' burn them slow.
According to the Celtic tree calendar there are nine sacred woods and within contemporary witchcraft and Wiccan teachings there are nine woods that should go into making the sacred fires. These woods are birch, rowan, ash, elder, willow, hawthorn, oak, holly, and hazel.

15 Elder be ye Lady's tree - burn it not or cursed ye'll be
Of the nine sacred woods listed above, elder however is considered the tree of the Goddess and should never be burned.

16 When the wheel begins to turn - let the Beltane fires burn.
Beltane (Bealtaine) is a fire festival that marks the gateway to summer. The balefires were lit as a means of cleansing and protection, as well as blessing and fertility.

17 When the wheel has turned a [sic] Yule, light the log an' let Pan rule.
Yule (Norse) is the time of the winter solstice. It is commonly known as the time when the Gods rule the land.

18 Heed ye flower bush an' tree - by the Lady blessed be.
    A reminder that Wicca (or contemporary witchcraft) is an earth-centric spiritual belief and as such we are guardians for the environment and land upon which we reside.

19 Where the rippling waters go, cast a stone an' truth ye'll know.
    Water divination is common amongst many pagan peoples. This line can also refer to other forms of divination.

20 When ye have need, hearken not to others' greed.
    Make sure your intentions for the use of magick are clear. Magick is a skill and a gift that does have consequences. Ensure that you are aware of these consequences and that they align with your personal ethics.

21 With the fool no season spend or be counted as his friend.
    Choose your friends wisely and a reminder to stay away from people with an overall negative energy.

22 Merry meet an' merry part - bright the cheeks an' warm the heart.
    Be grateful for your friends and family, and do not be afraid to express your love and gratitude for them.

23 Mind the Threefold Law ye should - three times bad an' three times good.
    The Threefold Law has been explained earlier.

24 When misfortune is enow, wear the Blue Star on thy brow.
    When you experience misfortunate or difficulties in your life, your third eye chakra (ajna) is located in the middle of your forehead) and connects you with the higher forces in the universe, including the Gods.

25 True in love ever be unless thy lover's false to thee.
Consider the vows you make. If you vow to love someone, be true to them. If they have been untrue (i.e., cheated, lied about who they really are, etc), then that breaks any vow made.

26 Eight words ye Wiccan Rede fulfil - an' it harm none, do what ye will.
It all comes down to those eight words which have been explained in depth in this chapter.

One's Highest Ideals

Within contemporary witchcraft, there is the concept of acting with respect to one's "highest ideal" as within the Charge of the Goddess, the Moon Goddess states:

"Keep pure your highest ideal; strive ever towards it;
let naught stop you or turn you aside."

A person's "highest ideal" can be likened to their "True Will" as found within the Thelemic magical tradition, where an individual, a follower of that path, acts in accordance with their Higher Self, one's Holy Guardian Angel. Within contemporary witchcraft, it means that as the neophyte grows spiritually, their horizons, personal limitations and preconceptions continuously expand and mature. This is because we each have embarked on the endless quest of spiritual self-discovery and learning.

In my tradition of contemporary witchcraft, the neophyte is given certain "passwords" to assist them along this path. These passwords are considered appropriate since they indicate unconditional (perfect) compassion (love) and wisdom (trust). They also provide a standard against which to measure actions, motivations and growth. Prior to initiation, the neophyte is expected to have meditated upon the phrase "Perfect Love and Perfect Trust" in order to understand its deeper meaning. Likewise, any person seeking entry into the inner court of a contemporary witchcraft coven is expected to fully understand, or at least give due consideration to, the words of the Goddess and endeavour to "strive ever towards their highest ideal," for this implies that as the neophyte grows within the Craft, their horizons, personal limitations and preconceptions will continuously expand and mature.

Whatever we believe in, our actions (just like our words or

thoughts) have a magical effect. They ground and concretize our morality (or lack thereof) in our daily lives. This grounding creates the habits and the environment that fuel and reinforce our future directions. If we claim to value compassion, personal responsibility and self-knowledge (in other words, to have a conscience), but we enact selfishness, self-indulgence, and constant emotional self-stimulation, it is these latter qualities that we will invoke into manifestation in our minds, and our environment.

Like any magical invocation, this is governed by two factors: firstly, what we are invoking (our ideals and conceptions of divinity), and secondly, the amount and type of personal energy that we put into it. Both these factors must be strongly present and aligned for any positive magical operation to succeed. Otherwise, we simply invoke our own negativities and hidden motives which we have clothed in a divine form (with the attendant results in our spiritual and personal lives).

Real magick and spiritual or religious maturity depends upon sincere and practical morality and insight. Often, morality demands that we have the discipline and capacity to overcome our laziness and work at things that we would not otherwise do. In magick, as in life, most things worth having must be worked for. It follows that a spiritual path worthy of its name must have precise transcendent ideals – that is, ideals that force us to go beyond our personal motives, concepts and expectations. Anything else is unworthy of being called a serious spiritual pursuit.

In contemporary witchcraft, when we cast our magical circle, we also invite into it our Gods. When we step into our magical circle, we are striving to become one with them as earthly incarnates of these higher powers in the universe, and as such, we humble ourselves before them. When we step into our magical circle, we perceive not only our coven brothers and sisters as being children of the Gods. We are reminded that the

Goddess loves all her children and as such, what we should be striving to do is to take this act of humility and compassion out beyond the circle, and incorporate it into our everyday lives. If we truly believe in magick, then we know that if we constantly think of someone in a certain way, that is how they will become, and that person also relates to our own self.

The underlying meaning of highest ideal is realising the ongoing obligation we have of demonstrating constant morality, self-examination, spiritual aspiration and deep concern for the welfare, development and happiness of others, regardless of their spiritual and/or religious persuasion. It is in acting upon this ongoing obligation of self-examination that we constantly strive towards our highest ideals, just as we are encouraged to do in the Charge of the Goddess.

True Will

As mentioned earlier, according to magician Aleister Crowley, every man and woman possesses a spark of the infinite divine potential, and that spark may be kindled into a shining star. As every star gives light and has its proper course in the cosmos, this combination of nature and motion is, in effect, the True Will, or the will of highest and divine self. Just as we have a moral obligation to pursue our own spiritual evolution, we have the same obligation to discover, and then do, our True Will.

There are some results that follow naturally from this way of thinking:

- Nobody's True Will can be in conflict with someone else's since both are part of the universal harmony and the infinite oneness.
- The inertia of the universe, the movement of the oneness, is behind the True Will of the Individual, since that Individual is part of that oneness.
- The inertia of the universe is opposed to actions which

conflict with the True Will of the person performing those acts (an explanation of "Threefold Law of Return").

- Each individual who realises and actualises their True Will makes it easier for others to do so, by increasing the inertial force of the universe.

Know Thyself

We are told that above the doorway to the temple of Apollo at Delphi, Greece, the words *Nosce temet* (a translation of *gnōthi sauton*, Greek for "Know thyself") were written. Followers of contemporary witchcraft have an obligation to their inner or higher divine potential to strive to know, understand, and to comprehend their divine nature. This brings about spiritual self-realisation, which enables the witch to then actualise that divine potential by bringing it into full manifestation in accordance with their own highest ideal or True Will.

In order for this to be achieved, the process of "spiritual alchemy" must be undertaken. The formula of the ancient alchemists was *Solve et Coagula* or to "dissolve and recombine". Contemporary witches should strive to examine their nature, character, and feelings, and to dissolve the neuroses and complexes which interfere with their own spiritual evolution. Mechanisms which were perhaps once necessary as a crutch to help the person survive and function, but have become counter-productive, must be transformed into more functional and productive methods of dealing with life's needs and interactions with others.

We must learn to forgive past harms at the hands of others, and of ourselves as well, in order to free ourselves of the emotional complexes which plague the "inner child" and bind us to non-productive or even harmful reaction patterns and behaviours.

Naturally, such a process is one that could take a considerable amount of time to achieve, if, in fact, it is at all possible to achieve the dealing with deep issues in one lifetime. However, the underlying aspect to this point is that the Craft encourages us to constantly strive for self-improvement, to act with humility and to be able to identify when ego is at play. Often our actions speak louder than our words. None of us are perfect, and even the most experienced witch is human, and therefore is subject to human failings. Something to bear in mind, especially if you happen to come across a teacher who claims otherwise.

Unlike many new age teachings, within contemporary witchcraft we recognise that the ego is a part of us, making up our personality. To "remove" the ego therefore seems to imply that we have no personality. What we should be doing instead however is to be mindful of when our ego is being dominant and unwavering. When our judgment is solely self-centred without any consideration for the consequences made or of other people and even beings. It is only natural to have some people disapprove or not like our actions, thoughts, opinions, etc. It is impossible to be able to please everyone, especially all of the time. However, we can be mindful of where we operate from and act accordingly. After all, this is taking self-responsibility and learning to act in accordance with our True Will as talked about earlier. When we are able to do this, then we are fully embracing the meaning of the Wiccan Rede.

Is Contemporary Witchcraft the right path for me?

Taking all of what that I have mentioned up until now on board, I suggest the next thing you should do is to pause and ask yourself: Why? If you are exploring a possible new religious or spiritual path, what you are actually looking for? After all, if you do not know what you looking for, how will you know if contemporary witchcraft, Wicca, or any other path is for you? Are you seeking a new spiritual path due to the failing of your current one? If so, then what exactly are these failings and where do they come from? An interpretation? The way they were taught? The teacher or religious adviser who taught them?

As an alternative belief system, paganism on a whole does tend to draw to it somewhat traumatised Christians who are often simply disillusioned with how their particular church has been run, as opposed to the teachings found within Christianity itself. In other words, they still have a belief in Jesus and the Christian concept of God, just not in their priests. As author and blogger Thorn Mooney[20] declared in one of her blog posts: "Wicca [or contemporary witchcraft] … is not a refuge for the religiously wounded." A statement that I wholeheartedly agree with.

Choosing a belief system simply because it is not one that you have an issue with does not do justice to either belief system. Nor will it provide you with the spiritual peace and meaning you are seeking. This is because you will find yourself comparing the two and preventing yourself from having the ability and confidence to explore and perceive contemporary witchcraft, or even Wicca, for its own merits. In other words, you should not make it your "rebound religion".

Instead you need to explore why you are no longer satisfied with Christianity, for example. If it is the church you belong to, then maybe explore another, or even another priest, or even denomination. If is the actual teachings found in the Bible, then that could be a more appropriate sign to start investigating other beliefs. Even then, you still need to know what you are looking for.

If you are drawn to contemporary witchcraft (and here I also include Wicca) because you perceive it does not have structure, hierarchy and protocol, then what you are attracted to is not truly the Craft. This is because it does actually have all these things, just presented in its own unique way. Once you discover this, because you have not dealt with your own issues with structure, hierarchy and protocol as a whole from your previous belief system, how do you think you will honestly react to these within contemporary witchcraft, or any other system? At the end of the day, it would be more beneficial for you to deal with your own issues, and previous negative experiences before attempting to transplant them onto a new belief system. From the point of view of someone who has run training circles for over 15 years, it is not uncommon to have people almost expect me, or my Craft, to be able to "magick away" their issues, often with little if any of their own input.

Mooney's advice is blunt and to the point: "Grow up and deal with your own life."

Back in the 1960s, traditional witch Robert Cochrane declared that "modern witchcraft could be described as an attempt by 20th century men to deny the responsibilities of the 20th century"[21] where it was being used by people as a means of escapism – whether it be their responsibilities or their problems. If this is what you are hoping, that contemporary witchcraft will provide you with a means to escape being an adult in the now 21st century, then you will be sorely disappointed. Both contemporary witchcraft and Wicca are about taking full responsibilities for areas of your life (financially, emotionally, and spiritually). So, you need to be conscious of your own progress, as there is no room in the Craft where you can hide from responsibilities in your life and blame others when things do not go according to your preference. From my own personal experience, as well as witnessing what others have gone through, the opposite often happens. The Craft tends to bring up all those deepest issues that we have been happily suppressing, for us to deal with once and for all.

As mentioned earlier, contemporary witchcraft and Wicca both contain within their teachings what can be described as a version of the "Golden Rule". In Christianity, the "Golden Rule" is "Do unto others as you would have them do unto you". Within the Craft, this is the Wiccan Rede, which states: "An it harm none, do what ye will" which advises that the path of least harm is the ethical path, and we should always think before we act. It also reminds us that we are to take responsibility for the consequences of our actions (as well as our thoughts and deeds), as well as the results when we fail to act.

Regardless of whether you belong to a group or are a solitary, once you commence your own personal investigation into the world of contemporary witchcraft and Wicca, you will soon realise that you need to become accountable for your own self. This means being solely responsible for your words, actions, thoughts and conduct, as well as even matters of the heart.

Further, the only real power that you obtain is that of self-empowerment and gaining a better understanding of yourself. If you are looking for superhero qualities to suddenly emerge from billowing clouds of incense smoke, then the truth can be rather disappointing. The magick which forms part of the Craft is often very subtle and unless you know what to look for, can go unnoticed.

Any spiritual practice should have periods of pushing your boundaries, of making you question and reconsider things – not only the teachings, but also yourself as an ever-evolving spiritual being. When contemporary witchcraft is practiced effectively and in the manner in which it is supposed to be, it changes us. That is its whole purpose. If you approach the Craft, or any spiritual path come to that, with the perception that it is the other way around, then you are in for some hard lessons.

It is about discovering a new and often fresh way to see the world around you and your place within it. It moves beyond teenage angst, acquiring a new set of magical tools, observing festivals dates, collecting skulls, crafting spells and declaring yourself to be a "witch" to anyone who will listen. It is about deeply analysing yourself and what is truly important through the exploration of nature, not just that of your own little world (microcosm), but also the cosmos around and beyond you (macrocosm). It is also about analysing our relationship with all that which arounds, and not just humans.

The teachings found within the Craft are not linear. While there may be a starting point for you (i.e., when you first venture onto the path), there is actually no starting or ending point in the teachings themselves. They tend to be cyclic, ebbing and flowing with the changing phases of the moon as well as the turning of the seasons. They are also "helical", i.e., having the shape or form of a helix much like a coiled spring, in that with each competed cycle you make (i.e., the turning of the seasonal Wheel of the Year), you gain more knowledge into the Mysteries. Therefore, while you may find yourself back at the place where you started, you have not actually returned to the same spot because of the knowledge and experiences gained on the way. This is because the teachings of the Craft are not something that can be turned off and on any more than going to church on Sunday makes you a Christian. You need to embrace and live the teaching, putting them into practice, as opposed to merely applying lip-service. It is when you put thing into practice that you gain a deeper level of understanding and connection.

Like all spiritual and/or religious paths, contemporary witchcraft and Wicca do not necessarily suit everyone, no matter how much people try to "water down" the concepts so that it fits nicely for consumption by the masses. There is also more to these paths than observing the seasons and phases of the moon. Contemporary witchcraft, in particular, is still very much today a "Mystery tradition" and, as with such traditions in more ancient times, often the mysteries gained are found within one's own self. It is for this reason alone that if you feel that this is the path for you, you should undertake various exercises to heighten your own awareness and develop your own natural abilities, including psychicism, for such cannot be gained from reading a book, only through the actual practice. Such Mysteries also only reveal themselves over time, often when you are least expecting it. The "aahh" moment is often used to describe a person's realisation of the Mysteries unfolding which they are now in a position to understand.

Before you go any further and start looking for a teacher, maybe you should ask yourself the following questions:

- What can contemporary witchcraft or Wicca offer me?
- Why do I want to become a witch or a Wiccan?
- What do I really want to learn from contemporary witchcraft or Wicca?

Once these questions are pondered carefully and answers given honestly, then you will be able to determine what the best spiritual path is for you.

From this self-analysis, you might like to consider the role that Christianity plays in your life. Regardless of whether you consider yourself a Christian or not prior to embarking on a study of the Craft, in the West, we live in a Christian-based society and as such, the essence of this belief has shaped our ideas, images, and philosophies. It also influences our ordinary conversations as well as underpinning our politics. We have seen this in more recent times in Australia when it comes marriage quality, abortion legislation or even euthanasia. In such instances the conservative right tends to flood the airways with their Christian morality. Yet it is interesting to note their eerie silence when it comes to the exploitation for financial gain, even to the point of the extinction of species or displacement of other humans, so that a minute few can benefit at the expense of others. To me, this seems more like paying lip serve to their religion as opposed to having any deep and meaningful relationship with their path and what it actually means to have such a spiritual belief.

One rather controversial way to "free" yourself from the impact that Christianity has on you is to recite the familiar Christian Lord's Prayer backwards. When I suggest doing this rite to students, it is not uncommon for some to experience a sense of uneasiness. Considering this act is what is often depicted in Hollywood movies as being an act of Satanic worship, such initial reluctance is understandable. As mentioned in the previous section, Satan has no place in contemporary witchcraft. If you find yourself questioning the rationale of doing this, then that is the point that I have mentioned earlier about the impact that Christianity has in shaping our lives even on a subconscious level.

Instead, as explained in his book, *Mastering Witchcraft*[22], Paul Huson refers to this rite as the "Releasing the Power of the Witch" as it enables breaking the subconscious "shackles" of our Christian-based society. It enables you to have a free slate upon which you can place your own set of morals and ethical codes. It is little wonder, therefore, that the Church is so against this rite and that Hollywood depicts it in such a manner.

My own version of Huson's rite can be found in the Appendix. I would recommend that you familiarise yourself with at least the standard ritual process prior to embarking on this rite. You should also journal your answers to the questions asked earlier in this section prior to performing the rite; journal how you feel afterwards, in order to form a benchmark for your own spiritual growth.

When to Dedicate or Initiate

Within contemporary witchcraft it is common to undergo some kind of ritual that marks your interest in and dedication to the Craft. If you belong to a coven, this usually takes form as an initiation, and within contemporary witchcraft there are three different levels of initiation. If you are a solitary, then the rite is a self-dedication. While the word "initiation" comes from the Latin *initi(um)* meaning "beginning", the dictionary meaning, and that used within contemporary witchcraft, is to undergo the action of being admitted by someone, through formal admission, into a group or society that keeps such knowledge. It is a ritual that marks the transition from being a seeker (an outsider if you like) to being formally recognized as a "proper" witch (i.e., in accordance to the teachings contained within contemporary witchcraft), a priest or priestess of the Craft, and a full member of the coven (i.e., an insider).

On the subject of initiation, there is still a great deal of secrecy surrounding what actual happens during the initiatory process despite Books of Shadows including Gardner's, being available online. This is because every coven that aligns to contemporary witchcraft will have their own particular "secrets" that enable the experience to be much more profound than what is initially assumed from an outsider's (non-initiated) point of view. After all, the experiences gain and how these are understood are often based on the teachings received and the personal interaction.

Dedication, on the other hand, is often seen as an alternative for a solitary practitioner with it being a personal rite between you and the Gods, and is defined as the act of setting apart and consecrating something or a person to a deity or for a sacred purpose. As such, the act of dedicating should not be taken lightly as the word itself is synonymous with "committed" in that its definition means "the quality of being dedicated or committed to a task or purpose". It is a declaration to yourself and the Gods that you have chosen to identify as a witch, and traditionally takes place a year and a day after you first commence your journey. While it is not essential that you have to wait this long, it is recommended that dedication should occur when there is no question in your heart that you identify as a witch and that the Craft is something serious to you that you love and respect. Once such a rite has been undertaken, it cannot be undone.

Some indications that you are ready to undertake a self-dedication rite are:

- Magick is real and you accept it as part of your life.
- You are comfortable with the notion of the Gods.
- You can take full responsibility for your own actions.
- You see yourself one with the natural flows of nature and the universe as opposed to a desire to gain control and gain domination over it.

Do you need to be dedicated or initiated to be a witch in the first place? The short answer is no. Once you have decided that this is the path for you, the Gods will endeavour to guide you should you be open to their signs and teachings. All you need to do is to step through the veil and open yourself up to the energies (these ancient powers) that lie beyond want we classify as "normal". This in itself creates a kind of inner "initiation" if only on a psychic or astral level. The truth be known is that if this is indeed the true path for you, you will know. Witches know they are witches. It is a gut feeling that is more than wishful thinking. This is because they have been witches in a previous life.

It is important to point out that the process of dedication or initiation tends to "seal" (or reaffirm) any previous connection of being a witch in a past life into the physical being that our soul has incarnated in this life time. This sealing is done through the power of the ritual undertaken, not just the physical act, but also on a deeper soul level.

If you wish to join a contemporary witchcraft coven then the opportunity to initiate will be offered to you if it is considered appropriate and you suitable. Initiation after all is a gift, a sign of recognition that you have reached a certain stage. You do not automatically have some holier than thou magical power bestowed upon you either. Once initiated, it is not possible to "un-initiate", and indeed there have been some initiates who have sadly chosen to abuse their initiation status as opposed to demonstrate the appropriate degree of humility that is expected.

There is a downside to walking the path of the witch. If your upbringing has been within an orthodox religion, you might find yourself in conflict, or even personal turmoil, with the conflicting values and teachings (which is why I recommend performing the "Releasing the Power of the Witch" rite). You may even find yourself being faced with the challenge of breaking away from your current life style, the safety of being accepted, in order to become an outcast, or living on the fringe of what was familiar. It is not uncommon to find you may find yourself with little, if anything, in common with people who have been friends with all your life. As such, you will be seeking to find another community of likeminded people.

With this in mind, if you have any doubts regarding your own commitment or whether this is the right path for you at this stage, then it may be best not to self-dedicate. If you chose the latter option, that should not prevent you from continuing your exploration of the Craft.

There is a dedication rite provided in the Appendix section should you feel that this is something you would like to do. Of course, you can use it as a template and add to it or alter it to make it more fitting and personal to you.

Understanding and Working with Deity

Central to contemporary witchcraft is the belief in deity. In order to properly understand this, I feel it is necessary to first discuss what deity is about, before moving into the specific belief that is found within the Craft.

The divine consciousness, universal energy, Great White Spirit, or whatever term you are comfortable in using, describes a force that is basically beyond our understanding on our current physical plane. In contemporary witchcraft, this energy manifests itself into masculine (the God) and feminine (the Goddess) aspects. Both these aspects are equally important, and form part of the divine consciousness (the macrocosm), as well as our own selves (the microcosm). Unlike other more orthodox religious or spiritual paths, one thing that quickly becomes apparent about the differing pagan traditions is the abundance of Gods and Goddesses, or deity. But why is this and how does one choose the most appropriate deity?

Humankind's earliest religious or spiritual beliefs would have depended very much on the environment in which they lived. For example, if a tribe resided next to the river, they would have specific deities associated with that particular body of water. A tribe residing in the shadows of a volcano would have, no doubt, deities associated with the powerful forces of the volcano. Most pantheons have certain deities associated with the basic needs and wants of their people: health, fertility, nature and of the hunt, etc. The more patriarchal tribes also had deities associated with warfare and victory. This is why when we look at the differing mythologies from around the world, we often come across various deities with similar yet, different, qualities, such as the various sky deities like Zeus (Greek), Thor (Norse), Jupiter (Roman) and Taranis (Gaulish).

There were even deities that were believed to have resided

in specific places, or acted as a guardian, patron, or protector of a particular place, geographic feature, person, lineage, nation, culture or even occupation. These deities were referred to as "tutelary". In ancient Rome, the tutelary deity of a man was his "Genius" while for a woman it was her "Juno" (also the name of the wife of Jupiter). Boann is the Irish Goddess of the River Boyne found in County Leinster, Ireland, while Pachamama is a Goddess, revered by the indigenous people of the Andes Mountains of South America, who not only presides over the planting and harvesting of crops, but who also embodies the mountains themselves, and causes earthquakes.

Today, our knowledge of differing deities allows the luxury of picking and choosing the ones we like best. Our ancestors, however, did not have this knowledge. If they were in Greece, they would have known only the Grecian deities; if in Peru, it would have been those of the Incas, and so on – until they came into contact with another race of people and their subsequent deities. An overlapping from matriarchal to patriarchal cultures also becomes apparent.

When one culture was taken over by another, deities of the first were often adopted or became, as is believed the case with many Goddesses, subordinate to the God of the conquerors - a wife, daughter, concubine, or even enemy. A prime example of this is the Goddess Hera. We have heard of the long-suffering and over-jealous wife of Zeus, the chief Grecian deity and Thunder God, but there is little awareness that Hera is actually a much older deity, who had a completely different role from that which we associate her with today.

Barbara Walker[23] mentions that Hera's name may have been "He Era", meaning "the earth", a later version of the pre-Hellenic Great Mother, Rhea. Both were forms of the Great Goddess of early Aegean civilisation, who predated the appearances of the other Gods. It was the Hellenic writers, therefore, who were said to have "married" this Goddess with the Olympian Zeus, and maybe their constant struggles reflect the conflicts between the early patriarchal and matriarchal people.

Other deities were blended to represent both the original culture and that of the conquering one. In Britain, for example, the Goddess of the healing springs of Bath in southern England was known as Sulis by the local Britons. However, after the conquering Romans, this deity became known as Sulis-Minerva, as the Romans often did not replace the original deities with their own.

Today, people tend to select a variety of pantheons depending on their own personal preference. But how do we do this? In order to understand the various deities, and discover how to interact with them more easily, we need to study them and strike up a relationship with them. Their stories can be found in the ancient worldly myths and legends, folklore, and even fairy-tales. Images can be found in art galleries and museums, and if we are lucky enough, we can visit the lands from which they came. Keeping in mind that when reading the stories, they might not necessarily be the original ones. As many traditions were originally oral, the stories have been translated, retranslated, and even watered down to fit morals of the time, such as during the recording of myths in the Victorian era.

Having said this, within the coven sense of contemporary witchcraft there are actually specific names by which deity is referred to which are oathbound and therefore not disclosed outside one's initiated tradition.

To the observer, contemporary witchcraft may appear to be a belief system that is based on theology, that is, the study of the nature of deity. While this may be the case, it actually goes beyond the study aspect and aims to teach the practitioner how to establish their own personal relationship with the Godhead, i.e., either their own chosen deity or the God and Goddess in general outside those used within a coven situation.

Joseph Campbell, a leading expert on mythology, is said to

have stated that "God is a metaphor for that which transcends all levels of intellectual thought. It's as simple as that." Those of us following contemporary witchcraft however tend to disagree.

Myths and Archetypes

When looking at the word "myth" itself, it tends to denote a narrative, or story, possibly comes from an older word meaning "to yearn for", "to think, to imagine". We therefore often tend to treat myths as fictional tales about the Gods and Goddesses, stories with no basis in reality. How, then, can a story appear and reappear in roughly the same form throughout different times and places in history?

The world of myth keeps the stories of deity alive. We read about the adventures, the trials and tribulations of these divine beings, and often can see similarities in our own lives. It is through discovery of the stories of deity that they become more than just faceless names on a page. They reveal to us that they are aspects of the universal energy, the divine consciousness, and so are we.

Our appreciation and interpretation of mythology, especially on a pseudo-psychological level, stems largely from the work of psychoanalyst Carl Jung, who, together with his followers, helped us understand the workings of the mind. The human psyche is neither rational nor logical. Its world is similar to the world of dreams: proverbial, non-linear, present tense, non-dualistic, multi-layered, multi-vocal, symbolic and polyphonic.

Myths represent a world of images that transform into other images in the blink of an eye, a symbolic world more comfortable with metaphor and poetry than with concrete facts, symbols serving as a bridge between the unconscious and conscious minds. In the inner world, emotions, feelings and states of mind become personified, represented as a person, God, Goddess, or archetype.

Accordingly, the Jungian archetypes are the building blocks

of the psyche, the organs of the soul. They are metaphors more describable by images than by words, entities easier to experience than describe. He likened the form of the archetype to the central system of a crystal, which preforms the crystal's structure even though it has no actual physical existence itself. Nonetheless, archetypes are dynamic, energetic, their representations more a snapshot than the living reality.

Archetypes are channels through which psychic energy moves; they are different possibilities of existence. We can experience archetypes as personifications: Gods, Goddesses or figures such as the Great Mother, the Wise Old Woman (or Man), the Divine Child. These entities are powerful images with their own life and energy; they have a fascinating, spiritual quality.

The archetypes are universal, existing at the level of what Jung called the "collective unconscious" - the symbols, energies and images that are available to all humankind but which are particular to an individual. This shared unconscious explains how the same story can appear in different cultures. Although the archetypes are universal, their expression is personal: they come into existence through personal experience. These personified forces are not human; they are impersonal, dynamic energy not able to be contained within an individual person.

We can be "possessed" by an archetype, so identified with it that the archetype, rather than our own conscious mind or will, dictates action. Mythology appeals because it contains archetypes: it is a true story about our inner world. Jung, writing at the end of his life, wrote that it is only through myth that we can express what we are to our inward vision.

Myths are told in the language of the psyche: dramatic, emotional, fantastic, symbolic, and metaphorical. A particular myth draws us because it contains symbols important to our inner world, figures that somehow resonate deep in our psyche.

Role of Deity in Contemporary Witchcraft

Within contemporary witchcraft, the deities we believe in are real. They go beyond the concept of archetypes as Jung perceived and manifest as entities in their own right. Although our personal experience can appear to be similar, the "inward vision" of Jung is often experienced externally.

All historical deities are facets of the divine in that they each represent someone's understanding of divinity, and all are valid in their own way. English occult writer and ceremonial magician, William G Gray explains it this way:

"So-called civilised man made a terrible mistake in supposing divine or other telesmic images to be nothing more than worthless figments of immature imagination, having no more behind them than purely human origins. Half a truth is worse than a whole lie. Man may formalise divinities of devils, but he cannot energise them. Their force must come from the entities they represent, and these are real enough in their own realm. Everyone formulates according to their own ideas."[24]

Gray goes on to state that:

"Whether we make up Father-Gods, Mother-Gods, Saviour-Gods, Nature-Gods, or the likenesses of our deceased ancestors, we provide some kind of form for the God that lies within us. There is nothing wrong, inaccurate or undesirable in the fundamental idea of constructing formalised expressions for the forces of entities beyond and behind our ordinary human state of being..."[25]

Thought forms of deity are a conceptual bridge between humanity and the unknowable ultimate. It helps us to put a human face on the divine, making it easier to relate to, and easier to see the divinity within ourselves. But of course, divinity resides everywhere, not just in people.

Within contemporary witchcraft it is understood that deity is in all things, not "out there" somewhere apart from nature. We talk about an immanent deity rather than a transcendent one. This theme runs through the Charge of the Goddess:

> "... If that which thou seekest thou findest not within thee, thou wilt never find it without thee.
> For behold, I have been with you from the beginning ...".

Ceremonial magician, Walter Ernest Butler, expressed the same idea in different words:

> "The ignorant man gazeth upon the face of nature, and it is to him darkness of darkness. But the initiated and illumined man gazeth thereon and seeth the features of God."[26]

Occultist Dion Fortune further stated that "the Gods are alive in the minds of all of us and it is up to us to open the channels of inspiration".[27]

In what sense are the Gods real? An immanent deity is not a matter of abstract belief, but something we experience and relate to in a thousand different ways every day. Pagan author Starhawk explained it very well. When asked whether she believes in the Goddess, she replied:

> "... The phrase 'believe in' itself implies that we cannot know the Goddess, that She is somehow intangible, incomprehensible. But we do not believe in rocks – we may see them, touch them ... . We know them: we connect with them. In the Craft, we do not believe in the Goddess – we connect with Her, through the moon, the stars, the ocean, the earth, through trees, animals, through other human beings, through ourselves. ... She is within us all."[28]

The process of describing, understanding and connecting with divinity is never-ending. The tools we use for this immense task are the names, images and stories of the Gods from many cultures and eras. For witches, no single image can convey the vastness and wonder of deity. "God" is too large to fit into so small a box. Therefore, monotheism does not work for us in the day-to-day practice of our spirituality. A blend of animism, pantheism, and polytheism does.

Contemporary witchcraft is a spiritual tradition that has a foundation built on the idea of unverifiable personal gnosis or knowledge of spiritual wisdom. Within Druidry, this is referred to as *Awen*, or "fire in the head". Gnosis relates to our personal knowledge and experiences which we hold as personal truth may not be able to be outwardly proven to others. In order to establish and nurture our relationship with the Gods, to gain personal enlightenment, or to seek the deeper understanding of the Mysteries, the witch is expected to experience moments of epiphany or gnosis when communing with deity. This can be achieved through meditation, contemplation or even ritual, and all are personal experiences that would not yield external proof, but would bring the witch who experienced them to a deeper understanding, a higher vibrational frequency, and balance.

One of the best ways to achieve unverifiable personal gnosis is to begin to connect and work with a chosen deity. This can be done a number of ways including the following:

- Read whatever material that you can find on them, i.e., myths and legends, other people's interpretations, etc. For example, if you have chosen a Greek deity then you may like to read the Orphic or Homer's hymns, while information about the myths of the Norse Gods can be found in the Eddas or the Sagas.
- Set up some kind of altar dedicated to that particular deity, or simply light a candle and meditate on connecting with

the deity. Be patient, as it may take a number of attempts before any connection is made. It is also recommended that you record your practice. See the section on journaling and keeping a magical diary.

- Make offerings to your chosen deity such as flowers, lighting candles and incense, leaving specific food items that they like – money, crystals and the like. What offerings to leave will be evident from your research into the chosen deity. Demeter for example, is the Greek Goddess of the grain, so a suitable offering would be to include some grain or bread (preferably homemade as opposed to standard store-bought). I have a small altar in my garden that is dedicated to Demeter as she is also assorted with the harvest, to encourage an ongoing abundance of vegetables.

- Recite sacred prayers or hymns that were once believed to have been recited to the Gods. For example, those relating to Greek deities can be found in the works of Homer or the Orphic hymns. Hindu deities often have their own specific mantras, as well as pujas (devotional services), with information about these practices being freely available on the internet. Lesser-known deities may be honoured through simply stating that you want to connect with them and letting yourself be guided by what you may feel or be drawn to.

When it comes to the God and Goddess of contemporary witchcraft, from a historical point of view, the God is traditionally associated with nature and wildlife. He often appears antlered (as a stag) or horned (a bull, ram or goat). As you will see in the section on the Wheel of the Year, the God does take on various guises throughout the year, yet all of these are interconnected through him being a reflection of nature. The Goddess, on the other hand, traditionally is associated with the moon, the stars and the cosmos. This tends to contradict the modern pagan association of a "Mother Earth" and "Father Sky" concept which possible originated from various indigenous peoples.

Spirits within the Craft

Aside from the Gods there are other beings or spirits that can be found within contemporary witchcraft. Within my particular tradition the concept of ancestors is important, and as such our Samhain ritual is very ancestor orientated. According to my teachings there are various interpretations of what ancestors are, from your own personal bloodline, spiritual tradition or even of the land upon which you reside.

- **Bloodline**: These are people from your family who have passed over and who you may wish to connect with. When a person dies, their energy "signature" remains the same as it was when they were alive. Their presence may be noted by scents or tastes that you associate with them. One time I found my mouth watering for a pot roast, and as the only person I knew who made mouth-watering pot roasts was my grandmother, I knew she was making her presence felt.
- **Traditional**: In this context I am referring to the ancestors of your teaching or initiation. For those who have been initiated into energy healing modalities like Usui Reiki for example, you are initiated into a lineage of practitioners who have gone before you. The same applies to contemporary witchcraft.

  If you are a solitary then there are also traditional ancestors that you can call upon for guidance and these are any characters that you may feel personally drawn too regardless of whether they have been an actual real person or not. Merlin, for example, has a variety of beliefs associated with him as to whether he actually lived or not. These beliefs however have in common the fact that Merlin is an extremely wise man, knowledgeable in the ways of magic and also healing. These beliefs add to the image of Merlin and within magical teachings, this image can be referred to as an "egregore", or universal pattern, rather similar to what Carl Jung called the "collective unconscious".

• **Land**: This refers to the ancestors that reside in and of the land upon which you reside, often associated with the First Nations people. In Australia for example the Aboriginal peoples had their own pantheon depending on "country" or family group, as well as some shared spirits, i.e., the Rainbow Serpent. It is believed that these land spirits are as achieve today as they always have been. If you are not comfortable calling on those ancestors by their chosen names, then you can call upon the spirit of the land itself. For example, Australia was once referred to as "Gondwanaland" so you could call upon those spirits of the land.

Ancestors and the Mighty Dead

Within contemporary witchcraft, one of the most important links that a witch can make is with the ancestors of their tradition. It is this link that creates the magical "family". Once this link is made through the process of initiation, it is not able to be severed except by the will of the witch alone. This is because ancestors are more than just names on a family tree. They are the guardians and guides who shape the practice of all contemporary witches, regardless of whether the practices are following the original format or have been slightly adapted for modern times.

Gardner referred to the ancestors of the Craft as the "Old Ones" of witchcraft or the Mighty Dead. In The Descent of the Goddess found within the Gardnerian Book of Shadows, Death instructs the Goddess:

"To fulfil love, you must return again at the same time and at the same place as the loved ones; and you must meet, and know, and remember, and love them again. But to be reborn, you must die, and be ready for a new body. And to die, you must be born; but without love, you may not be born."[29]

American witch, M Macha Nightmare[30], describes the Mighty Dead as:

"… those practitioners of our religion who are on the Other Side now, but who still take great interest in the activities of witches on this side of the Veil. They have pledged to watch, to help and to teach. It is those Mighty Dead who stand behind us, or with us, in circle so frequently."

In contemporary witchcraft, ancestors are often referred to as the Mighty Dead a term that refers to the witches who have passed over including Gerald Gardner, Doreen Valiente, Alex Sanders, and Stewart Farrar.

The Mighty Dead can also refer be a person full of wisdom and knowledge in ancient times, i.e., King Arthur. They may also be one of your direct ancestors, e.g., if your grandmother was an herbalist and knew how to heal then she could be classified as one of the Mighty Dead.

Differences between the Hemispheres

As the origins of contemporary witchcraft are based in the Northern Hemisphere, practitioners south of the equator often find themselves at odds as to what to follow – the traditional teachings that do not tend to resonate with the land here in the Southern Hemisphere. To be told, as I initially was, that no change was needed except to "simply move the sabbats around" highlights a lack of understanding of the differences between the two hemispheres. To counter this, and considering I live in the Southern Hemisphere myself, I thought I would include my thoughts on how I personally equate this difference into my own practice. It may also be of interest to readers in the Northern Hemisphere to feel that the traditional teachings do not work in their environment.

Over the years, I had aligned my practice more and more to reflect the land where I reside in order to work more in alignment with these energies. While this action may raise questions, especially from those practitioners who are more traditional in their approach, for me it deepens my understanding and appreciation of the Craft's Mysteries; not to mention that at times it presents a challenge.

There are five basic differences between the Northern and Southern Hemispheres that any practitioner of contemporary witchcraft residing south of the equator needs to take into consideration. These are:

- **The Seasons and Sabbats**: This, of course, is the most obvious, as there is the marked six-month difference in the seasons. This is because of the 23° tilt the earth has on its axis. When it is summer in the Northern Hemisphere, it is winter here in the Southern Hemisphere. It is for this reason that the seasonal symbolisms associated with

Easter and Christmas are out of place here in the Southern Hemisphere. While in the following section we look at the mythos of the Wheel of the Year, a more in-depth information about working with the Southern Wheel can be found in my book *Dancing the Sacred Wheel*.[31]

Earth

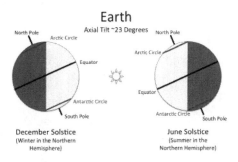

December Solstice
(Winter in the Northern Hemisphere)

June Solstice
(Summer in the Northern Hemisphere)

- **Direction of the Sun**: The tilt of the earth's axis also means that while in both hemispheres the sun rises in the east and sets in the west, on its journey across the sky in the Southern Hemisphere, it travels via the north. For this reason, most pagans in the Southern Hemisphere cast their circles in this direction, via the north, or in an anti-clockwise direction as opposed to via the south, or clockwise.

According to the *Australian Concise Oxford Dictionary*, the word *deosil* comes from the Gaelic deiseil meaning "sunwise" or "in the direction of the (apparent) motion of the sun". In Scottish folklore, deosil was considered the "prosperous course". The word *widdershins* comes from the Middle High Germanic word *widersinnig* meaning "against" and "sense", also "in a direction contrary to the apparent course of the sun". In Scotland, it was the lowland Scots (from East Lothian down to the English border) who favoured the word widershins. In more modern times, the association with clock direction has been included.

To assist neophytes who attend my training circles, I

prefer to use the terms "deosil" and "widdershins" when it comes to circle-casting and moving about the circle as opposed to clockwise and anti-clockwise which is commonly used in books and on internet sites. Neophytes are encouraged to consider when the first watch was invented (approximately the 18th century) in relation to the use of the words describing the journey of the sun across the sky.

- **Earth's Energy Flow**: In the Southern Hemisphere, energy moves in a widdershins, or anti-clockwise, direction while in the Northern Hemisphere, it is deosil, or clockwise. This energy movement is due to what is known as the Coriolis Effect that is due to the earth's rotation. The Coriolis Effect also impacts upon ocean currents and weather patterns, making storms swirl deosil (clockwise) in the Southern Hemisphere while they swirl widdershins (anti-clockwise) in the Northern Hemisphere.

- **Placement of the Elements**: Traditionally we are instructed that east is the direction of air, south is fire, west is water and north is earth. This placement is generally adopted throughout the Northern Hemisphere, however, it does not necessarily reflect the energies south of the equator.

When looking at the placement of the elements logically, as the sun rises in the east, this is why many magical traditions position the element of air in the east. Air represents new beginnings, and this is reflected in the rising sun. With the sun setting in the west, the element of water (which rules the emotions) is often placed in this direction. It is the placement of fire and earth that are usually change by people residing in the Southern Hemisphere.

Environmentally, where I live, to the north is the equator and from the north come the scorching summer winds. North is also the placement of the noonday sun so it would seem logical for the element of fire to be placed in the north. It is from the south that the sun never appears in the Southern Hemisphere, and it is the direction where the bitter cold winter winds blow from. It is, as well, where the frozen mass of Antarctica can be found. Therefore, the element of earth is placed in the south.

Having said this, you feel that these elemental placements do not reflect your natural environment then you are encouraged to observe your own local environment in order to see what works best for you. For example, if you live on Australia's eastern seaborne (i.e., Sydney), water may relate to east (representing the Tasman Sea or Pacific Ocean). Alternatively, if you live on the west coast (i.e., Perth), west might relate to air (the direction that winds blow across Australia from the Indian Ocean) while east relates to earth (the rest of the Australian continent).

Even if you reside in the Northern Hemisphere, I would suggest that you consider whether the traditional placements reflect the environment where you live.

- **Phases of the Moon**: The final difference is the directions of which the crescent of the waxing and waning moons point. In the Northern Hemisphere the waxing moon points to the left while the waning moon points to the right. These images are reflected in the symbols we often find of calendars for the waxing and waning moons. In the Southern Hemisphere however this is not the case as the waxing moon actually points to the right while the waning moon points to the left. This means that for those of us living south of the equator, not only should the symbols for the moon in our calendars be changed, but also the symbol of the Triple Moon Goddess (the Maiden, Mother and Crone) which is often depicted as somewhat extroverted in appearance (with the horns pointing outwards), while in the Southern Hemisphere it is actually introverted in appearance.

There are times, however, when the moon decides to really throw the spanner into the works and the waxing moon can be observed at times lying on her back pointing upwards, and the corresponding waning moon pointing downwards.

The Seasonal Wheel of the Year

The turning pattern of the seasons within contemporary witchcraft is known as the "Wheel of the Year". Each aspect of seasonal change is understood as a mystery of the divine. As the Wheel turns, so nature reveals the many faces of the Gods. In shaping rituals to express what we see and feel at these times, we share in the mystery of the turning cycle and join more closely with the vision of the God and Goddess. The following information has been adapted from my book, *Dancing the Sacred Wheel*[32] which explores the sabbats, in particular how they relate to the Southern Hemisphere, as well as their historical connection and ideas of how they can be observed in these modern times.

There are eight festivals, sabbats, observed throughout the year, each of which begin at sunset and last to sunset the following day in alignment to how the ancient Celts marked their observances. The sabbats are usually broken down into two groups. Four of these festivals are commonly considered to be Celtic in origin and agriculturally based. They mark the beginning (or "gateways") of the seasons and often referred to as the "Greater Sabbats" (or "Cross-Quarter Days" as they occur at the exact mid-point between a solstice and equinox):

Imbolc – beginning of Spring
Bealtaine – beginning of Summer
Lughnasadh – beginning of Autumn
Samhain – beginning of Winter.

The remaining four, the "Lesser Sabbats" (or "Quarter Days"), are largely solar festivals as their timing is determined by the relationship of the sun to the earth. These are the solstices and the equinoxes. Throughout its yearly journey, the sun makes four clear divisions: at the solstices (the longest day and the longest night) and at the equinoxes (when the hours of darkness and light are equal). Together, these form an equal armed "solar cross" and mark the midway points between each of the Greater Sabbats. The four festivals that make up this solar cross are:

Winter Solstice – the shortest day
Spring Equinox – equal day and night
Summer Solstice – the longest day
Autumn Equinox – equal night and day.

When the two sets of sabbats are combined, they make two equal armed crosses or an eight-spoke wheel (the Wheel of the Year). This symbol can be found repeated, not only throughout paganism with varying associations and meanings, such as emphasizing a circular sense of time through the seasonal festivals, but also within other spiritual belief systems, such as Buddhism and Hinduism as the *dharmachakra*, the "Wheel of Law".

The dates given below are general dates for the festivals in both the Southern and Northern Hemisphere, taking into account that the ancient Celts celebrated their festivals from dusk to dawn the next day.

	Northern Hemisphere	Southern Hemisphere
Winter Solstice	20 to 23 December	20 to 23 June
Imbolc	1 February	31 July to 1 August
Spring Equinox	20 to 23 March	20 to 23 September
Bealtaine	30 April	31 October
Summer Solstice	20 to 23 June	20 to 23 December
Lughnasadh	1 August	31 January to 1 February
Autumn Equinox	20 to 23 September	20 to 23 March
Samhain	31 October	30 April

When the astrological timings are taken into consideration, the sabbat dates can occur up to two weeks after the calendar dates. This may actually reflect the seasonal changes better with respect to the sabbat.[33]

	Northern Hemisphere	Southern Hemisphere
Winter Solstice	0 deg Capricorn	0 deg Cancer
Imbolc	15 deg Aquarius	15 deg Leo
Spring Equinox	0 deg Aries	0 deg Libra
Bealtaine	15 deg Taurus	15 deg Scorpio
Summer Solstice	0 deg Cancer	0 deg Capricorn
Lughnasadh	15 deg Leo	15 deg Aquarius
Autumn Equinox	0 deg Libra	0 deg Aries
Samhain	15 deg Scorpio	15 deg Taurus

There are corresponding seasonal myths associated with each sabbat. As all myths tell a story, the Wheel of the Year mythos tells a story of the God and the Goddess, but also of our own lives. While these myths are based in the Northern Hemisphere, it is important to understand their symbolic nature in order to gain a deeper understanding and appreciation of the sabbats themselves. Once the symbolism behind the myths is understood, we can then apply it to our own lives, in order to attune to the cycles of nature on a deeper, subconscious level.

Many pagan traditions begin the Wheel of the Year with Samhain, the Festival of the Dead. This idea originates in Irish Celtic tradition and works well when talking about the journey of the God.[34] However, we will start by looking at the seasonal wheel at the winter solstice, being the birth of the God.

Winter Solstice (Yule)
Northern Hemisphere - 20-22 December
Southern Hemisphere - 20-22 June
The winter solstice celebrates the concept of renewal and rebirth during the darkest time of the year, the time of the longest night.

Also referred to as "Yule" (pronounced EWE-elle) that comes from the Nordic word *iul* meaning "wheel", or the Feast of the Promised One, this is the time within contemporary witchcraft when we celebrate the return of the waxing sun. It is the darkest time of the year, the time of the longest night, yet there is the promise of the return of light and life and the conquering of death. The winter solstice is a turning point, a point of change, where the tides of the year turn and begin to flow in the opposite direction.

Within contemporary witchcraft, the God represents the sun and has journeyed into the Underworld at Samhain waiting to be reborn. As such, the winter solstice could be seen as belonging to the Goddess who will bring forth the new Sun God, the Child of Promise or "divine king" who is born cloak in the greens of the forest, and who, in turn, brings light, warmth and fertility to the land.

With the rising of the sun comes the promise of spring, and while it may still be a long time before the sun/son will be strong, we know that this will occur. The sun, as the Child of Promise, is the young hero God. It is a time of making wishes and hopes for the coming year, and of setting resolutions. From the darkness comes light.

Imbolc, Oimelc

Northern Hemisphere – 31 January-1 February
Southern Hemisphere – 31 July-1 August

Early spring is Imbolc (pronounced IM-bullug or IM-bulk) from the Irish Gaelic for "in the belly" (of the mother) while the Scots Gaelic word for this sabbat is Oimelc (pronounced EE-mulk) for "ewe's milk", referring to it being lambing season. In the Northern Hemisphere Imbolc occurs around 1 February, the sacred day of the Celtic Goddess Bride (pronounced "Breed") or Brigid.

This sabbat represents the quickening of light and life as around first stirrings of spring begin to appear. These seeds which have lain dormant within the earth over the cold winter months now begin to stir with life.

Within contemporary witchcraft, both the God and Goddess are becoming aware of their powers of potential. The young God is also beginning to understand his sacred purpose and is initiated into the mysteries of his sex. He is the young stag god – playful, inquisitive and adventurous, yet somewhat naïve as to his role in the greater cycle of life. As he pounds the earth with his hooves, and his light warms the cold earth, he calls forth the promise of fertility and life. The Goddess is renewed from her mother aspect and is reborn as the Flower Maiden. She is aware of her powers of potential. She is unrestrained and full of the energy of youth. She is also the huntress and the athlete and can be identified with Diana or Artemis.

As we celebrate the waking of the soul, our spirits begin to quicken as we anticipate the rebirth of nature. It is time to put action behind our thoughts and desires in order to start turning these into realities. In some traditions of witchcraft, Imbolc is the traditional time for initiation or the reaffirming and reflecting upon the oaths that you have made.

Spring Equinox (Ostara, Eostre)

Northern Hemisphere - 20-22 March
Southern Hemisphere - 20-22 September
This festival is named after the little-known Anglo-Saxon Goddess Eostre (pronounced OHS-truh or EST-truh), who was also known in Old German as Ostara (pronounced o-STAHR-uh). All that was known about Eostre was that her festival was celebrated around the spring equinox. This has been interpreted as possibly being a forerunner to Easter.

The spring equinox is a time both of fertility and new life, and of balance and harmony. Light and dark are in balance, but the light is growing stronger. It is a time of birth and of manifestation as we witness the new growth and swelling buds on the trees as

Persephone returns from the Underworld, to be reunited with her mother, Demeter, again.

Within contemporary witchcraft, the young God merges into his role as the hunter/warrior, testing his strength and his masculinity while the Goddess patiently waits, growing with her passion and power. All around them the earth is carpeted with flowers and new green growth. In some traditions this is also the time when the Dying and Resurrected God returns to the land.

Bealtaine (Beltane)

Northern Hemisphere – 30 April-1 May
Southern Hemisphere – 31 October-1 November

Bealtaine (pronounced BELL-tane) Irish Gaelic, and is similar to the Scots Gaelic *Bealtuinn* (pronounced bee-YAWL-tinnuh or BELL-tinnuh) meaning "Bel-fire", named after the Celtic God of Light being Bel, Beli or Balor. Bealtaine marks the start of summer and is a time for feasting, merry-making, celebration and joy. Druids kindled great bale fires on the tops of the nearest beacon hill. These need-fires had healing properties, and people would jump through the flames to ensure protection or drive their cattle between two such bonfires before taking them to their summer pastures.

Within contemporary witchcraft, the Goddess and God are now in full bloom of young adulthood. In the glowing sun, the sprouting green and the tender coloured blossom, they celebrate the fulfilment of their passion. This is the sacred marriage of the Goddess as the land, with the young God as the force of life in his guise as the Lord of the Greenwood, in the full vigour of his manhood. The traditional colours of the Maypole ribbons represent their sacred union with white, representing the semen of the God, and red, for the menstrual blood of the Goddess.

Bealtaine is also the time when the veils between the worlds are thin and when the fae are about. Folklore states that if you scatter flowers around the house, they will keep the fae away. Or if you washed your face in the morning dew, you will not get sunburnt in the summer or get wrinkles.

Summer Solstice
Northern Hemisphere - 20-22 June
Southern Hemisphere - 20-22 December
At the summer solstice, the sun is at its peak and the earth is revelling in the fulfilment of love. Flowers are in bloom, ready for pollination, fertilisation; yet once fertilised they die in order for the seeds and fruits to develop. At the same time, summer fruits appear, for a short but delicious season. All around us, life is a hive of activity.

Within contemporary witchcraft, the God has fought the powers of darkness, and is triumphant, ensuring fertility in the land, as the Sun God. But in so doing, he sows the seeds of his own death. As such, we also celebrate life, and the triumph of light, while acknowledging death. The Goddess shows her death-in-life aspect as while the earth is fertile and the flower is in bloom, once fertilised, they will die so that the seeds and fruits may develop.

Although from this point the days begin to grow shorter, the time of greatest abundance is still to come. The promises of the God and Goddess are still to be fulfilled. This is a time of beauty, love, strength, energy, rejoicing in the warmth of the sun, and the promise of the fruitfulness to come. It seems a carefree time, yet the knowledge of life is the knowledge of death, and beauty is but transitory. We celebrate life, and the triumph of light, but also acknowledge death.

Lughnasadh (Lammas)
Northern Hemisphere – 31 July-1 August
Southern Hemisphere – 31 January-1 February
In Irish Gaelic, Lughnasadh (pronounced LOO-nah-sah) is a feast

to commemorate the funeral games hosted by Lugh in honour of his foster mother, Tailte. For that reason, the traditional Tailtean craft fairs and Tailtean marriages (which last for a year and a day) were also celebrated at this time. This festival is also known by its Saxon name Lammas (pronounced LAM-mus), meaning "loaf mass" where the first loaf baked from the newly gathered corn celebrates the corn harvest. Cattle markets would be held and goods traded, all in preparation for the coming winter.

Within contemporary witchcraft, the Goddess at Lughnasadh is the bountiful mother as well as the Crone, wielder of the sickle. Lughnasadh is known as the first harvest festival. The God is both the Stag God as well as the personification of the spirit of nature, the Corn King, who is cut down with the harvesting of the corn. Amidst all the abundance, the Goddess mourns his death, but she knows his blood and body will feed the land. As she is with child, she knows that the God will be reborn again at Yule, the winter solstice.

Lughnasadh is considered a time of thanksgiving and the first of the three pagan harvest festivals. The sun's strength begins to wane and the plants of spring begin to wither and drop their fruits or seeds for our use as well as to ensure future crops. At this time, we become conscious of the sacrifice the Sun God is preparing to make. We experience a sense of abundance. At the same time, we begin to feel an urgency to prepare for the death of winter.

Autumn Equinox
Northern Hemisphere - 20-22 September
Southern Hemisphere - 20-22 March
The two equinoxes are times of equilibrium. Day and night are equal and the tide of the year flows steadily, but whilst the spring equinox manifests the equilibrium before action, the autumn equinox represents the repose after action, the time to take satisfaction in the work of the summer and reap its benefits.

This is the second harvest festival, both grain and fruit having been gathered in. We celebrate the abundance of the earth, and make wine from the excess fruit, to preserve the richness of the fruits of the earth to give us joy throughout the year. This is the time of the vine. Within contemporary witchcraft the God, who was Lord of the Greenwood in the summer, and the Corn King at Lughnasadh, now dances his last dance upon the earth, as Dionysus, God of Wine, before making his descent to the Underworld.

The God's presence is shadowy. His face is turned towards the Underworld, yet he is heard in each sigh of the wind and glimpsed in the shades of early dusk. He leads us to the hidden, inward places of our souls and invites us to explore. As the autumnal equinox marks the completion of the harvest, and thanks giving, with the emphasis on the future return of that abundance.

Samhain
Northern Hemisphere - 31 October
Southern Hemisphere - 30 April
Samhain (pronounced SOW-wane) is the death festival, marking the descent of winter. The leaves are falling from the trees in drifts, and life is drawn away from the surface of the earth. It is a mysterious time, belonging neither to the past or present.

The Horned God has taken his throne as the Dread Lord of Shadows, the comforter of souls, the guardian of the portals between the land of the living and the realms of the dead. We say farewell to him until the time of his birth at the winter solstice. The earth prepares for rest and draws energy inwards. This is a time for introspection, as we draw our energy within and prepare for winter. The earth is becoming cold and barren, and we see her as the Cailleach, the Crone, the Wise One. She is the Dark Mother who devours the God that she may give birth to him again. Her womb is also the tomb, and the Underworld, and the Horned God thus resides within her womb over the winter months.

Within contemporary witchcraft, Samhain is a sombre time when we remember and honour those who have passed through the veil that resides between the world of the living and the world of the dead. As this veil is at its thinnest, deceased ancestors and spirits are communicated with and invited to join in the sabbat observances.

The Wheel now turns back to the winter solstice with the birth of the Sun God.

Mabon and Litha

As a side note, in my tradition of contemporary witchcraft, I do not refer to the autumn equinox as "Mabon" nor summer solstice as "Litha" as, contrary to modern perception, neither words actually have any historical reference to either the associated equinox or sabbat. While this is explained in more depth in *Dancing the Sacred Wheel*, it was American author and witch Aidan Kelly who, in the 1970s, first associated "Mabon" as an alternative to the autumn equinox after Mabon ap Modron, a character who appears in Welsh folklore (*The Mabinogion*) despite him being more appropriately connected with the sun. He also associated Litha with the summer solstice allegedly inspired by the *Lord of the Rings*[35] where "Lithe" was referred to as the name for midsummer's day in the calendar for the fictional race of Hobbits. Kelly's reasoning for doing this at the time was that these two festivals did not have a Celtic (or Norse as is the case of Yule) name. Despite this pseudo-history, or "fake news", it is disappointing to notice that an increasing number of pagans, even those following contemporary witchcraft, continuing to use "Mabon" and "Litha" due to these historical inaccuracies.

Part II

Practical

The Importance of Journaling

What better way to commence the practical section of this book than to talk about the practical art of journaling.

The energies that we work with within contemporary witchcraft are often extremely subtle, as is our progression along this path when it comes to developing our magical and psychic abilities. From the outset, therefore, it is highly recommended that you get into the habit of journaling or documenting your work, regardless of whether you may feel that nothing has happened. It is often only in hindsight when you look back from where you once were to where you are now that you will be able to accurately grasp just how far you have progressed.

Your journal or magical diary is your work book, and it is different from your magical grimoire or "Book of Shadows" (talked about more fully in a later chapter). Also referred to as a "Book of Mirrors", your magical diary is an important item because it serves several functions, namely:

- To indicate your progress, as the subtle changes one undergoes may only become clear with hindsight.
- To check the effectiveness of practical magick you have performed, by detailing rituals and spells, and writing results which occur and critically relating them to causes.
- To be a private space for examining and questioning yourself honestly without the influence of ego-bias, a place where doubts and questions can be freely expressed, and all the psyche's shadows allowed to come into light.
- To express creative insights as they occur in life, helping you to see the cycles that tend to occur, and thus helping development by using them positively and directing energies appropriately.

You should attempt to practice at least some of the exercises every day as you work through this section. At first, they may seem to take longer to perform. However, as you become more familiar with the techniques, the speed and effectiveness with which you can perform them may surprise you

Writing also improves your memory of a given situation and also helps you to clarify events after they have happened. Therefore, recording your workings in detail is also very useful should you have to substitute items or if you are experimenting (with care) with different techniques. You should also keep in mind that the ultimate goal is not speed, but being able to perfect the techniques and achieve the desired end result.

In your magical diary you can record the books you have read and any interesting quotes or passages that you may like to further research at a later stage, and snippets of conversations you have engaged in or listened to, from podcasts and YouTube videos. You can also record your own personal thoughts about what various elements of contemporary witchcraft may mean to you, any dreams or symbolisms that you have come across, and the like.

As this section includes various exercises for you to undertake, recording your progress with these exercises in your magical diary would be highly recommended. Similar to a normal everyday diary, it is recommended that you should make daily entries in your magical diary. To do this, you may like to keep it by your bed to journal before you go to sleep each night. If this is not possible, then you should endeavour to make entries at least a couple of times per week and on a regular basis. Making regular entries in your diary help to develop self-discipline.

For each entry in my own magical diary I include the date, what astrological phase the moon is in, what I did ritually, and my thoughts afterwards. Flicking back through some of my earlier diaries, I have also included notes from tarot and psychic readings that I had had, brochures from workshops I was interested in, and even pamphlets from psychic and fairs that were of interest to me at the time.

Regularly journaling is a great way to record dreams whose meanings may be revealed at a later stage; readings, and even the outcome of rituals and spells undertaken.

Meditation and Visualisation

Developing and enhancing your meditation and visualisation skills is essential within the practical side of contemporary witchcraft. However, without being able to master either technique, casting a circle or obtaining the focus needed to spellcrafting would be futile. Therefore, I believe these are basic foundation abilities for any witch.

An online dictionary meaning of meditation refers to being engaged in an act of "contemplation or reflection" as well as to "engage in mental exercise (such as concentration on one's breathing or repetition of a mantra) for the purpose of reaching a heightened level of spiritual awareness".[36] From a more magical perspective, medieval grimoires or other like texts do not appear to indicate such techniques being used, save for prayer. This tends to indicate that magick, and indeed the practice of witchcraft, can certainly be performed without meditation. Despite this and considering the overall benefits that meditation can bring to the individual alone, I hold the view that the practice of meditation is included to one's magical practice because it brings it to a completely different level.

Without focusing too much on the overall health benefits of regular meditation practice, the benefits for the magical practitioner can be equally as immense. Meditation is the concentration on a single stimulus, using an image or absence of one, the repeated action, the use of chanting (*mantra*), or rhythmic breathing (*pranayama*). It is a means of achieving an inner peace, a transcendental experience, a deeper insight, which can help in daily life and in the search for meaning. The technique of meditation was devised and still exists to assist the practitioner, to uncover within their own self that deeply hidden centre of the one creative life. From that centre, much can be understood that is obscure, and from that level, much can be done for the world.

Through the discipline of meditation, any time that you find yourself becoming distracted from your focus, you are able to return to that point. This builds a knowledge of your own mind and mental process that will greatly aid with discernment: Discerning another voice from your own mind (i.e., that of spirit, deity, even your spiritual guide or higher consciousness), and discerning fantasy wishful thinking from real contact with the higher forces in the universe.

The use of meditation within contemporary witchcraft is similar to that found within yogic and other practices in that it is a technique used to hone the mind into single-pointed focus (*dharana*). Even if you do nothing else, meditation can be seen as a critical facet of not just magical training, but basic life training in dealing with the pressures of modern living, especially if you suffer from anxiety or depression. The form of mindfulness involved brings you back into the present. Our mind can be described as being composed of three parts:

- **Conscious Mind**: What occupies your awareness at a given time.
- **Preconscious Mind**: What you can recall in an instant (such as the day's events, or details of your house).
- **Unconscious Mind**: The store of your experiences and knowledge.

Meditation usually connects you fairly immediately to the preconscious mind, and then more slowly to the unconscious mind. This opening to the unconscious is of tremendous value in coming to know yourself and finding your direction. It enables us to access, learn and come to understand the ideas and symbols it brings us.

Meditation is about focusing, self-understanding, and being able to see through your own negativity and false truths in order to "demanifest" your own self-imposed negative internal programs, instead of attempting to manifest them outside yourself using witchcraft. It can also improve every single area of your life by developing your mind, calming your emotions, and therefore, ultimately allowing you to transcend your ego in order to experience pure ecstasy.

The control and knowledge of mind also helps in being able to shift into different states of awareness so that a gigantic "let's break reality" evocation to physical appearance is not necessary every single time you want to talk to the Gods or spirit you have a relationship with. If you consider magick as more than just communication with the Gods, spirits, your Holy Guardian Angel or even higher consciousness, but a process of initiation and unfolding towards divinity, then how much more important is this process?

Meditation can be a difficult practice to master, even more so in our "ever-ready" instant world. It is also a skill that tends to be dismissed by novices of witchcraft and magick as being "non-magical", especially when the preference is placed on the physical external "doing" as opposed to the non-physical internal "listening". Yet meditation is often a foundational technique that is used within the practice of magick itself, when our focus is turned inward and the external distractions dissipate. It is an under-estimated technique that can also provide deeper reasoning behind the purpose of why the external ritual is being performed in the first place.

As mentioned earlier, in Eastern traditions, meditation is often coupled with *pranayama*, or being able to control of breath. In Sanskrit writings, *prana* is breath or the vital energy in the body. On subtle levels prana represents the *pranic* energy responsible for life or life-force, and *ayama* meaning "control". Therefore, pranayama is "control of breath." One can control the rhythms of pranic energy with pranayama and achieve healthy body and mind.

When it comes to meditation, one erroneous instruction made

by Western teachers is to "clear the mind" or to "think about nothing at all". Both of these things are near impossible, as the conscious mind is always thinking about things. The best advice is to give it something to think about, like counting the breath. The following Four-Fold Breath exercise does just that as well as assisting in learning to meditate.

Before undertaking any meditation technique, it is important that you sit in an appropriate position. If you regularly practice yoga, this can be the half and full-lotus position. It can also be sitting on the floor with your legs crossed or having your legs straight out in front with your back against the wall. A further adaptation is the "hero" position, where you sit on a straight-backed chair with your palms resting comfortably on your thighs, much like an Egyptian pharaoh as opposed to the yogic position of the same name. In yoga the "hero" position (or "Virsana" as it is known in Sanskrit, from *vira* meaning "hero") is to sit with your thighs perpendicular to the floor, feet slightly wider than your hips so that your buttocks touch the floor. If you can sit is this position comfortably then do so.

Regardless of how you sit, the most important thing is for your spine to be as naturally straight as possible and that it should be a position that you are able to hold comfortably for a period of time.

Exercise: Four-Fold Breath

This simple, yet highly effective, technique is most beneficial in calming and grounding you not only in your preparation for meditation and rituals, but also in your mundane life as well, when you need to become less stressed or anxious, and need to focus. It can be used to calm and centre the mind and body, as well as open the auric field in preparation for magick and meditation. It is important not to strain during this exercise and that you keep the body relaxed. If you feel any discomfort or dizziness, then stop the exercise immediately and return to your normal breathing.

The Four-Fold Breath technique can be used prior to any other meditation practice. In ritual work, I use this technique prior to casting my circle as a way of grounding and centring that allows me to clear my mind of the mundane tasks. This in turn enables me to focus on the magical work that I am about to undertake.

- Breathe deeply, yet comfortably, into your diaphragm for a count of four. Your stomach should expand and there should be limited expansion in the top of your chest.
- Hold your breath for a count of four.
- Exhale slowly and with control for a count of four insuring that you expel as much air from your lungs and diaphragm as possible.
- Hold your breath for a count of four before repeating the cycle.
- Repeat this exercise for at least 10 complete cycles. When you have finished, record your experience in your magical diary.

The objective is to ensure that your inhalations and exhalations are constant. If you find that you are not able to hold your breath for a full count of four, then reduce it to a count of two. Likewise, if you find that you are able to hold your breath for longer, then increase the ratio to one that you are comfortable with. Your counting of the breath and pausing should be constant.

A good counting technique is to simply use your hand and move your thumb up each phalange (section) of your finger as you complete a breathing cycle. Starting from the base phalange of your little finger and moving your thumb upwards and then across in a clockwise direction, at the completion of 10 cycles, you should end at the base phalange of your ring finger. Use your other hand to count each cycle of 10 by moving your thumb up each phalange as described above.

Alternatively, you can purchase a mala (that specifically has 108 beads) or even make your own set of counting beads. Examples of meditation counting beads, as well as other devotional beads, can be found on the LunaNoire Creations online etsy store[37].

With practice, with each deep inhalation and exhalation you should be able to settle into the self and be able to intensify your awareness of place. This will allow trivial cares to recede from your consciousness. Just breathe and be.

Exercise: Body Awareness

Having a basic awareness of what is "normal" for your body can be used as a benchmark later on, especially if you find yourself working with spirits, guides or even getting into trance work. Knowing your "normal" is also beneficial when developing or heightening your use of your own intuition of psychic abilities.

The objective of the following meditation is a form of mindfulness where you become aware of your physical self. If at any time during this exercise you find your mind wandering, just simply allow yourself to refocus on your breathing.

- Get yourself into a comfortable seated position. Close your eyes and focus on a simple aspect such as your breathing, the natural inhalation and exhalation process as you breathe.
- Slowly bring your awareness to various parts of your body, beginning with your feet. Imagine that your feet are the roots of your body, drawing awareness up from the ground up into the rest of the body.
- Allow this awareness to spread up through your feet to your ankles, calves and shins, to your knees. Notice if there is a change in temperature or whether your lower parts feel much heavier or looser than normal. If they do, then this is okay. If they do not, then this is okay as well.

- As you continue to breathe, bring your awareness over your knees and into your upper legs, hips, buttocks and genital area. If you find that you are holding tension here, then that is okay, as many people do. Imagine that particular area relaxing as you inhale and exhale.
- With your breath, continue moving your awareness up your spine, from the base all the way up to the top at the back of your skull. Relax with each breath that you take and ease the muscles around the whole of your head including your jaw-line.
- When your spine is relaxed, bring your awareness to your shoulders, adjusting them if need be so that they remain comfortable. Then draw your awareness down your arms and into the fingers.
- Once your hands and fingers are relaxed, slowly bring your awareness back up to your throat and release any tension that you may be holding there, before moving further up to your face. Notice how sensitive your face is, how the air feels against it.
- Finally bring your awareness to your brain and become aware of just how amazing and powerful your brain is. Your brain is capable of regulating your entire body. Your brain houses your mind which allows you to think, feel and create.
- When you feel ready, open your eyes and return to waking consciousness. Record your experiences in your magical diary.

With practice, with each deep inhalation and exhalation, you should be able to settle into the self and be able to intensify your awareness of place. This will allow trivial cares to recede from your consciousness. Just breathe and be in the present as much as you can.

An alternative practice to the above is to gradually increase your awareness to focus on the sounds around you. As you listen, you will become more aware of these sounds, and the effect they have on you (whether they are soothing, or irritating). Become aware of any peripheral sounds, which you do not consciously hear, but which are always there. Try to just listen without analysing.

Ideally, you should aim to meditate for around 30 minutes in the morning before going about your daily tasks as this will set you up for the rest of the day. If you have never meditated before, then it might be ideal to join a class or focus on the breath (such as in the Four-Fold Breath and Body Awareness exercises). While there are also numerous guided meditations available on CD or via YouTube, it is recommended that you aim to master focusing and controlling your mind without external stimulus.

Visualisation

Being able to not only visualise the circle that you are casting, but also the desired result of a spell, is extremely important when it comes to contemporary witchcraft. After all, visualisation has been described as being a meditative technique by which a witch formulates their desired magical result in their mind's eye.

Visualization is an important step between thought and conception. It is the process of purposefully creating images in the mind to bring forth into manifestation either consciously or unconsciously. As such, it can be likened to being a blueprint for your magical goals, detailing exactly what it is you wish to achieve. Learning how to visualise goes hand-in-hand with learning to concentrate, creating self-discipline, developing an active and controlled imagination, astral projection and dream working. All of these are important facets in the developing of your magical ability from casting your first circle through to the most complication spell creation.

Visualization is the creation of a pattern or picture within the mind and the holding the image while projecting it as a visual experience. While we are all able to visualise, the objective when performing magick is to be able to hold that visualisation for a set period of time to enable enough time and energy to be given to enable the manifestation of the desired outcome. The following exercises are designed to help you to regain and control that innate ability.

Exercise: Enhancing Your Visualisation Abilities

- Think of a subject which is important to you, i.e., building your dream house or visiting a particular place. Focus all of your attention on this subject, seeing in your mind's eye the house, the place. This is visualisation. The image in your mind's eye may waver or disappear at this realisation. The goal is to refocus and the image in your mind's eye for as long as you are able to. Record your progress in your magical diary.
- After you have successfully completed the first exercise and have been able to consistently visualise the subject or scene every day for a week, sit down in a room within your home where you have peace and quiet and let yourself relax. Focus on an object in the room, i.e., a chair, keeping all of your thoughts on that object. Notice any shadows, wrinkles in material, the grain of the wood, and so on.
- When you feel you have focused enough, close your eyes and attempt to bring the image of the chair into your mind's eye. Experiment with this object every day until you can do it and hold it at least five minutes, recording your progress in your magical diary as you go. After you have achieved holding the image in your mind's eye for at least five minutes every day for a week, then you might like to attempt the next exercise.
- Continue using the same object that you have been visualising on. Bring an image of the object into your mind's eye and hold it there. The objective of this exercise

is for you to be able to open your eyes and see the object before you (the image in your mind, not the physical object), placing it at eyelevel against a solid-coloured wall, preferably white in colour. Practice this for a week, recording your progress in your magical diary.

• The final aspect to this exercise is to change the colour of the projected image that you have visualised against the wall. You may like to practice changing the object to different colours and back to the original colour. Alternatively, or as an additional exercise, you might also like to visualise raising and lowering the projected object, turning it around and even upside down. Remember to record your results in your magical diary.

Visualization is not all that difficult, but it does require time, dedication, quiet and patience to master. When you are able to visualise, your rituals and spellcrafting will become more focused and therefore will be more effective. Visualization of the goal achieved, combined with the direction of the magical energy, will channel more energy, thus achieving a more effective ritual or spell working.

Exercise: Kim's Game

This game is commonly played with young children as a way of promoting the development of memory and observation. It is derived from a 1901 novel by Rudyard Kipling, where a British teenager (Kim) spends a month in British India at the home of a Mr Lurgan where he is secretively trained as a spy. Each day, Lurgan brings out a tray with various items on it. Kim's task is to count and remember what items were displayed after they were covered up.

Lord Baden-Powell, founder of the scouting movement, considered this technique to be an important part of observation training and included it in his book of games. Up to 15 items were placed on a tray and uncovered for one minute. Players then had to list as many items as they could, with the winner being the person who remembered the most items.

- Gather together at least 10 items on a tray. They do not have to be magical; random household items are perfect. Some examples are: a pen, teaspoon, box of matches, a crystal, tee-light candle, coin, clothes peg, small kitchen knife, a paperclip and business card. Once you have selected the items, cover them with a tea towel and leave for about 30 minutes. If you do not have a tray, you could use a shoe box.
- After about 30 minutes uncover and observe the items on the tray for a minute before covering up again. Then record as many as you can. Uncover the tray again and see how successful you are.

Variations of this game could be including the people who you share your household with, e.g., get a housemate, sibling or even parent to assemble the items. You may like to increase the number of items on the tray. Be more descriptive in your recollection (what colour crystal, what was written on the business card, etc).

Exercise: Strengthening Your Visualisations

- Ground and centre yourself by using the Four-Fold Breath technique.
- Close your eyes and imagine you are looking at a white wall or blank screen. Practice visualizing first with simple geometric forms – a line, circle, triangle, ellipse etc. When you are able to see the forms clearly, visualise the screen in colour – yellow, blue, orange, green, violet, black in turn. It may help to look at a coloured object with opened eyes first, then close eyes and immediately try to see the colour.
- Practice visualising the geometric forms with the colours.

Change the colours and forms until you mentally see them all at will. Download images from the internet or cut some from magazines if you are not able to draw them yourself.

- The next version to enhancing your visualisation ability is to visualise a piece of fruit, say an apple, with all its blemishes.

- Remember to record your results in your magical diary even if you feel that nothing had occurred. You will not always receive visions or experience major sensations. The energies that we work can be very subtle. That is why "knowing thy self" (i.e., what your "normal" is) is important, as you may experience subtle sensations including heat or coolness, prickling of the skin, slight touches and so on.

The Magical Power of a Witch

The most important mindset to have when practicing magick is faith – an unwavering belief in what you are doing, in your ability, and that your magick will work.

Witchcraft and magick go hand in hand. The 19th century magician, Aleister Crowley defined magick as "… the Science and Art of causing change to occur in conformity with Will". Modern occultist David Rankine explained that magick is "consciously directed energy flowing towards evolution. By extension, magical techniques can be seen as practical ways of creating positive change in the self and the environment …".[38] He goes on to say that when magick is used as part of a person's own spiritual practice, it enables the practitioner to directly experience personal gnosis or mystical experiences as opposed to relying on faith alone. It is through this personal experience that magick dares the practitioner to grow, not only magically but spiritually as well.

There are three internal practices that the witch needs to master within their own self, prior to being able to successfully craft magick, whereby the results are experienced externally and physically. These are:

- **Imagination** (to act) – this comes through visualisation,
- **Focus** (to concentrate) – being able to hold an image and/or thought/intention when needed and not being a scatterbrain (monkey mind), and
- **Passion** (to believe and make real). According to Hermetic magician Benjamin Rowe[39], "passion is the sense of an intense desire to be connected to that which you are seeking to invoke, a desire that places no restrictions or limit on the connection, but which is so one-pointed

that nothing save that which is sought is included in its focus."

The above three internal practices can be seen enacted by children playing games such as "Cops and Robbers" in that while the children realise that it is a game, they actually throw themselves into this realm of make believe in order to make it real. Therefore, when we step between the worlds, we need to believe 110% in what we are doing, in the purpose of the ritual, and in magick itself. Any doubt that we may have, not only in the practice but also the process, diminishes what we are trying to achieve.

Witch Power

Power within contemporary witchcraft denotes a sense of control. As such, it is often associated with having "power over" another person or being, as opposed to having "power with" with respect to having power within one's own self, i.e., self-discipline and self-control. Power is the action behind change. If there is no power, no drive, then there is no magick.

It should be remembered at all times that with power comes responsibility. If your reason to study contemporary witchcraft and the magical arts is to make yourself more powerful because you feel powerless, then the true objective of your desire to learn is to have power over other people. This power is often short-lived and can be weakened by fear and insecurity because you will constantly be in fear that someone else will take the power away from you. All this does is render you increasingly paranoid because you see magick as external and separate to yourself.

On the other hand, however, if your interest in these practices is to gain a better understanding of your own self, self-knowledge and self-awareness, then this is taking power within. When you understand the power within your own self and how to create it, you realise that no-one is able to take this power away from you (unless you allow this to occur). In other words, you become the power, you become the magick and it becomes integrated as part of you.

Energy is power. When we focus our intent, our energy, whether it is through visualizing a circle is being cast, or the desired outcome of a spell that we are crafting, we are focusing our innate power. It is for this reason that meditation and visualization are taught earlier in this course. Their importance within contemporary witchcraft and the other magical arts are often overlooked and even discredited today. Yet much power comes to the witch who has mastered these two skills.

The true power of the witch come from within. It is not connected with specific herbs and crystals, magical implements or other "distractions". It is the witch's intent, focus and belief in their ability. The ancient Delphic axiom of "Know Thy Self" echoes true even in the 21st century.

Survivor of the Auschwitz and Buchenwald concentration camps, and Nobel Laureate, Elie Wiesel, stated that "Ultimately the only power to which man should aspire is that which he exercises over himself." A witch seeking true power is a witch seeking to know their own self.

Power comes from the discovery and mastery of our own unique talents. When this is realized we further discover that each one of us, regardless of whether we are a witch or not, has everything within our own ability to thrive in this life. Every one of us has the capability of wielding incredible amounts of power and shaping our lives into whatever we chose to be. Yet we do not do this largely because of fear. We have been "taught" from an early age to give our power away, or even that there are limitations to what we are supposed to believe in or desire for ourselves. As we get older, we are constantly "taught" about what we are supposed to want and desire.

Take a moment and ask yourself what is it that you truly desire? What is it that your soul truly craves for? What is it that your heart truly desires? Are these the same things or different? You might like to record your thoughts in your magical diary as something to reflect upon.

It is important to understand that the energy we talk about in contemporary witchcraft is real. It is the same energy that energetic healers use. This is often the means through which spirits communicate with us.

Keep in mind the words of Salem witch, Laurie Cabot[40]:

"A witch's work is mind work and utilizes powerful metaphors, allegories, and images that unlock the powers of the mind."

The Eight Ways of Making Magick

Within the teachings of contemporary witchcraft, there are eight ways of raising energy or power to use for magical purposes which can be used on their own or in any combination in order to product more power. In Gerald Gardner's 1957 Book of Shadows[41] he referred to these as the "Eight Fold Path". Each of these eight ways are also meant to build upon each other, with the more advanced (and sometimes dangerous) techniques reserved for the end. They are:

- **Meditation or Concentration**: In simple terms concentration on a subject is the most basic form of raising and sending energy whereas meditation is a deeper form of concentration, and can be enhanced through specific postures and gestures. Gardner advised that while these paths can be combined, meditation or concentration was essential for all. He further advised that "if you have no clear picture of what you wish and no certainty you will not succeed".

- **Trance states, Clairvoyance, Projection of the Astral**: Ultimately, all forms of making magick should bring the witch into a state trance, albeit some may be lighter in nature than others. It is through trance that we are able to perceive the different realms and where we are able to manipulate the energetic links that connect things. Projection of the astral body is a technique taught in several ways depending on tradition of witchcraft including utilising carefully constructed pathworkings as well as the use of ointments, potions, or even shamanic techniques.

- **Drugs, Wine, Incense**: Of all the eights ways, Gardner cautions the use of these ways, noting that they are "dangerous and therefore if possible, should be avoided". The exception being the use of incense. Entheogens however have a long history in the Craft where they have been used in flying ointments, transformation elixirs, herbal incenses, smokes, anointing oils, washes and much more. Many substances are dangerous, and several of them are also illegal so it is wise to tread with caution. Wine alters the state of conscious and can be used as a gentle way to let slip the ego and find yourself outside of consensus reality when used in moderation. Caffeine can also create the same effect, as does using one particular incense for an extended period of time.

- **Dance, Performing Rites with a Purpose**: Possibly the oldest form of celebration and communication, and is often central to rising the cone of power within contemporary witchcraft. The "grape vine" step is often used within pagan circles, and in larger groups, the circle danced can spiral in to a central point and out again. Performing rites with purpose relates to the amount of intent and passion the witch puts into their magical workings.

- **Chants, Spells, etc**: A power of the spoken word can be used in a number of different ways as a form of raising energy. The words of a carefully worded chant can reinforce the intent of the magick, or they can be seemingly nonsensical words with traditional meaning.

- **Blood Control (Cords etc), Breath Control**: While Gardner does not warn against the use of cords to restrict blood flow, I feel it is appropriate to mention that this technique (known as "warricking") should be used under the guidance of someone who has been properly trained in knowing how to use cords to slightly restrict blood flow to certain areas of the body while the bound person is made to stand or sit in uncomfortable positions. Cords generally are used in knot magick where they form a focus of contemplation. Controlling the breath has been covered earlier in "Meditation and Visualisation".

- **The Scourge**: Used with a light stroking motion to encourage blood flow into certain areas. The light, rhythmic application of the scourge can produce trance just as would a steady drumbeat.

- **The Great Rite**: This is the act of sexual congress between two consenting adults who have each invoked a God or Goddess. Another term for this act is the *hieros gamos* or the playing out of a marriage between a God and a Goddess. What Gardner was actually getting at by including this as one of the ways of making magick was the ideal of sexual energy being used as a conduit for magick. For the solitary practitioner, this would naturally include masturbation.

Of all the possible combinations of practices, Gardner suggests that a combination of meditation/concentration, dance or performing rites with purpose, using chants and spells, and the use of the scourge is the best.

There are also five things that are needed in order for the witch to succeed in magick within contemporary witchcraft. These things are:

- **Intention**: You must have the absolute will to succeed, the firm belief that you can do so and the determination to win through against all obstacles. This is what Gardner was referring to in the act of "performing rites with a purpose".

- **Preparation**: You must be properly prepared; have everything you need ready for use once you cast your circle.
- **Invocation**: The elementals, and the Gods and Goddesses, be invoked into your circle.
- **Consecration**: Your circle must be properly cast and consecrated and you must have properly consecrated tools.
- **Purification**: You must be purified, both body and mind. More information as to how to do this can be found in the basic ritual provided in the Appendix.

What is Energy?

In the previous section, I have just indicated that power is energy. Maybe I have jumped ahead of myself and should explain what energy actually is. The word "energy" is derived from the Greek *energos,* meaning "active". Everything in the physical world, including all human activity, is a result of this vital, dynamic quality of life. In the original 1977 *Star Wars* movie, legendary Jedi Master, Obi wan Kenobi tells the hero, Luke Skywalker, about the "force" which is "an energy field created by all living things. It surrounds us, penetrates us. It binds the galaxy together." Such a description is so accurate in describing what energy is that you may have already come across it. The late Wiccan author Scott Cunningham extended upon this by defining energy into being three different kinds of "power":

- **Personal Power**: Resides within each of us and is generated within our own bodies.
- **Divine Power**: Comes from the Gods.

• **Earth Power**: Is generated from the earth.

Within contemporary witchcraft energy (power) is what we use to bring about change – that is magick. Therefore, it is important to either believe in the powers above, or at least have an open mind to the fact that energy exists, even if at first it seems to be all "make believe". As the saying goes, sometimes you need to "fake it" until you "make it." Within contemporary witchcraft this can relate to "make believing" before your conscious mind accepts that there is, indeed, another reality beyond the mundane and cannot explain away everything that happens. When things start to happen and your conscious mind struggles to make sense of it all, it is because you are "stepping between the worlds", as the saying goes – the mundane world and the non-mundane.

Energy Following Thought

Simply put, your thoughts trigger your emotions and your emotions determine your experience. Energy therefore follows thought. This is a metaphysical belief involving vibrations that have found its way into modern pseudo-psychology practices, such as "NLP" (neuro-linguistic programming). As your emotions establish your vibration, it is your vibration that attracts things into your life.

A thought always precedes an emotion, although for most of the time we are not aware of this process. This is because unless we are deliberately focusing and using our intent, our mind is filled with random and automatic thoughts. All that needs to happen is for our mind to attach itself to one of these random thoughts and our whole day, or even perception of life, can change. The Law of Attraction tells us that if we think positively, then we will "attract" positive things into our lives. Likewise, if we think negatively. Within the realm of magick, this is known as "sympathetic magick" (where like attracts like) or even the Law of Correspondence.

Through being aware of your thoughts and, more importantly where they originated from, you are able to gain greater control over your life and indeed your own personal power. All the voices in your mind are the result of opinions, judgments, jingles, beliefs, sound bites from the media, and the like. Start paying attention to what you are telling yourself on a daily basis. Write all these thought and opinions down. What is the energy that you are creating about your own self? How are you directing your power?

It is through understanding and utilising (or manipulating) that power of thought that with the practice, you are able to manifest things in your life. After all, this is how spells work.

Exercise: Awakening the Energy

- Begin by finding yourself a comfortable seated position. Ground and centre by following the Four-Fold Breath technique.
- Start to observe how you are feeling. Do you feel alert? Aware? Excited? Calm or anxious? Tense or relaxed?
- Bring your awareness to your spine and to the energy that travels up and down your spine. Your breath moves the energy in and out of your body. It awakens your body's energy centres, the chakras. As you breathe deep into your diaphragm, continue to notice how you are feeling, how your body is feeling. Do you notice your energy changing?
- There are seven major energy centres, or chakras, in the body, and while these are not technically part of contemporary witchcraft training, include them in my teachings due to my background in metaphysics and yogic training. Many people are familiar with the concept of chakras.
- Focus on your crown energy centre (*sahasrara*) that aligns us with the cosmos above us, and your base energy centre (*muladhara*), located at the base of the spine that aligns us

with the earth beneath our feet. As you inhale, visualise that you are drawing the grounding energy from the earth beneath you up into your body through your feet, and the cleansing energy from the cosmos down from the heavens above into your body through the top of your head. These two energies meet at your heart centre (*anahata*), where they intermingle and then circulate around your body as you exhale.

- As you continue to breathe, take note of how you and your body is feeling. When you are finished, record your experiences in your magical diary.

Exercise: Sensing the Energy

There are minor chakras located throughout the body included the palms of the hands. These chakras can become activated during energy exercises and energetic healing.

- Rub your hands together briskly and then slowly move your hands together until they almost touch, and then apart again. Repeat this process for about a minute. You should start to feel a sensation of resistance when you bring your hands together.
- Hold your hands over a crystal, rock, or even a flower. Take note of any sensations that you may feel and record these in your magical diary.
- Take special note if there is a difference between your hands. It is commonly believed that for a right-handed person you receive energy through your left hand (the less dominant) and give energy through the right (dominant), and therefore for a left-handed person the opposite is the case. Does this apply to you? Records your findings in your magical diary.

Exercise: Grounding Yourself and the Energy

- Sit in a comfortable seated position with your feet on the ground. Ground and centre by following the Four-Fold Breath technique.

- Close your eyes and bring your awareness to your heart centre (*anahata*). Feel your energy there and as you breathe, gently imagine or visualise the energy moving down your spine. The energy transforms into a tap root or cord that then extends down deep into the earth beneath you. If you like, imagine the tap root or cord being wrapped around a large rock deep within the earth.

- With each exhalation that you take, the energy descends into the rock. With each inhalation you take, the nurturing energy from the earth rises up through the golden cord to the base of your spine, where it then flows out to your whole body.

- Repeat the inhalation and exhalation visualisations for at least a minute or until you feel grounded.

- When you are finished, record your experiences in your magical diary.

Exercise: Candle Visualisation

- Place a lit candle in front of you either at eye level or on the floor. Settle into your seated pose as you take several conscious, slow, deep breaths before commencing the Four-Fold Breath.

- Let the eyes soften and relax as you gaze upon the candle flame. Notice any sensations you feel. Let your attention rest there for as long as feels comfortable.

- When the eyes grow tired, gently close them and bring the image of the candle flame behind the eyes or to the point between the eyebrows. Visualise the flame at that point. When the image of the flame fades, then allow the eyes to softly open again.

- Continue the practice of gazing at the flame and then closing the eyes and holding the image behind the eyes (or the point between the eyebrows). Observe how you feel. Let the practice be fluid. If it helps you in calming the mind, then adopt it as your own. Play with it and find a way to use it in your own life.
- Record your experiences in your magical diary.

The Magical Circle

Since ancient times, circles have always been of spiritual or magical significance, and evidence of this can be seen in the stone circles found throughout Britain, Ireland and across Europe. These circles of stones were raised with a sense of reverence for the land and an awareness of its inherently spiritual power. They were believed to have been constructed as places of worship, ritual and healing. Since the time of ancient Babylon, circles were drawn around the beds of sick people and mothers who had just given birth to protect them from negative influences, evil spirits or demons. A Roman ambassador, in a foreign country, would even draw a circle around himself with his staff in the belief that he would be safe from attack.

Within contemporary witchcraft, the magick circle is the temple wherein acts of honouring the Gods or magical rites are undertaken. It is a psychic space that is created as a gateway for the conscious to move between the mundane and psychic reality. Therefore, it is often considered foolhardy, and even at times dangerous, to cast a circle without correct knowledge and understanding of one's intended actions. This is because from the first moment that you begin to lay out your circle, certain factors are released to strike at triggers deeply rooted in your subconscious.

When we construct a circle within contemporary witchcraft, we do so to contain and focus the energies that we are dealing with in a structured manner. We need to contain these energies in order of us to use and interact with them.

Occult scholar and author Donald Tyson[42] described the characteristic of a circle as being able to separate what is inside of it from what is outside of it. Contained within the circle is order and control, while outside is anarchy and chaos. When it comes to magick, a circle is used as a wall of protection to divide the greater hostile world from the zone of law. The most obvious magick circle, according to Tyson, is that of the human body.

The witch, regardless of what tradition they may (or may not) be aligned with, uses the magical circle as a way of limiting their power in order to concentrate it and render it effective. In other words, the circle assists in defining and focusing their True Will. They have created a miniature world (the "microcosm") in which the witch becomes the ruling deity. This, in effect, upsets the natural balance of things as the circle becomes a magick sky palace and the witch can therefore be limited to the sun around which everything revolves.

It is important to remember that the physical circle is only a model upon which the witch may fix the real circle of the magical arts. It has little or no power at all until it is charged by the practitioner, who traces upon the physical circle a mental circle drawn upon their powers of visualisation. It is for this reason that developing your powers of visualisation to the extent of almost physical manifestation is so important.

When the circle is visualised out through the centre-point of the witch and mentally projected upon, it is visualised floating in the air at the level of the heart before expanding both upwards and under the feet, creating a sphere. This astral circle, is visualised directly above any physical representation of the magick circle which the witch may have previously drawn on the ground or floor. When joining the beginning to the end, the practitioner should take are that these two ends meet, for if the circle is not completed, Tyson advised that the forces of chaos may be able to enter.

Casting the Circle

According to Gerald Gardner:

"Power is latent in the body and may be drawn out and used in various ways by the skilled. But unless confined in a circle it will be swiftly dissipated. Hence the importance of a properly constructed circle. Power seems to exude from the body via the skin and possibly from the orifices of the body; hence you should be properly prepared."[43]

To be "properly prepared", this meant training and being initiated into a coven. Due to information being more easily accessible today, self-training is often considered to be sufficient outside more traditional forms of contemporary witchcraft. However, we still need to be in the right frame of mind, be cleansed and purified before creating a ritual. This is because within contemporary witchcraft, we are creating a sacred space into which we call our Gods, to witness what we are doing. Our circle becomes the holy of holy places, and as we will be in the presence of our Gods, we also need to be "holy", i.e., being "properly prepared". It is for this reason that specific clothing (robes) and jewellery is worn that is set aside only for when we are performing ritual. The wearing of street clothing, that is everyday clothing, is often considered inappropriate within formal contemporary witchcraft circles. This is because the wearing of specific clothing and jewellery items assists us in getting into the right form of mind that enables us to step between the worlds. They will often retain the magical energy that we are creating during our rituals. If you are interested in joining a traditional coven, then there is a strong possibility that you will need to have some kind of robe. Instructions for making a simple robe can be found in the Appendix of this book. For a solitary practitioner, however, normal street clothes are considered appropriate (as long as they are clean).

The circle is the basis to magical work. It symbolises wholeness, perfection and unity. It offers a boundary to hold the energy created for the specific working, as well as preventing to keep unwanted spirits or energy out. The circle also acts as a doorway to the realm of the Gods. Within the circle, it becomes possible to transcend the physical, and to open the mind to deepest and highest consciousness levels.

A witch's circle is a focus of earth energy as well as a symbolic representation on earth of the motion of the heavens and cosmos. Like all magick, it involves a combination of the heavens and earth; as Hermes Trismegistus stated: "As above, so below, as without, so within". When we cast, or visualise, a circle, we are attempting to create a microcosm, which contains all that is found in the macrocosm. Therefore, we ensure that we follow the energies of our physical location; we also ensure that we follow, as our ancestors did when they constructed the stone circles, the motions of the cosmos.

Regardless of our spiritual path, the circle symbolises the concept of wholeness and balance, cosmos and infinity. It is an outward expression of our conception of divinity, of wholeness and balance, and infinity. Like the Greek serpent, Ouroboros, perpetually devouring its tail, a circle has neither a beginning nor an end. It therefore conveys the notion of timelessness and perfection, and infinite inclusivity. That is, they symbolise the entire universe. Magical circles are therefore mini universes, just as I have mentioned earlier.

In circle casting, the term *deosil* does not mean "clockwise", as is mentioned on numerous internet sites and even in books. It actually means "with the sun". Although in the Northern Hemisphere this may be clockwise, the same does not apply south of the equator. Because of the tilt of the earth, the sun in the Southern Hemisphere makes its journey from the east to the west via the north, as opposed to the south as it does in the Northern Hemisphere. The sun, therefore, moves in an anti-clockwise direction between sunrise and sunset. As the basic idea behind casting a circle is to move with the sun, to tap into its power and strength, deosil in the Southern Hemisphere is therefore done in an anti-clockwise direction. Likewise, the term *widdershins* does not refer to the "anti-clockwise" direction.

It means "against the sun" and therefore, in the Southern Hemisphere, this is clockwise compared to anticlockwise in the Northern Hemisphere.

Within contemporary witchcraft the majority of cycles are cast deosil, with the sun. This is because we want to raise our awareness and consciousness. However, there are occasions when a widdershins circle is cast and these are:

- Any ritual that requires us to go within, i.e., for deep soul reflection and contemplation.
- Observing sabbats during the darker parts of the year, i.e., particularly Samhain and the winter solstice where we journey inwards to meet the God.
- Working with darker or more primordial aspects of deity who tend to reside in the Underworld.
- To banish or remove things that might be restricting us.
- Working with the dark phase of the moon.

Widdershins is also the direction used when we begin to call back the circle at the end of the ritual if it has been cast deosil.

Within contemporary witchcraft, a magical circle is traditionally nine feet (approximately three metres) in diameter. However, for the solitary practitioner it can be as large or as small as your space permits. When I commenced my journey with the Craft, I was living in a share house, so my only space was in my bedroom where I utilised a small area of floor that probably was no larger than a metre. This meant that when I cast my circle, I was virtually turning around on the spot.

The actual act of casting a circle requires 50% mental ability and 50% physical ability. It requires you to draw upon your skills of visualisation in that the energies that you are sending out are constructing a circle in your mind's eye, or psychic space. My initial teaching was to visualise this energy as cobalt blue in colour. Other people visualise an iridescent white or even a golden colour. At the end of the day it does not really matter what colour you visualise the energy as being. What is important is your ability to "see" (visualise) this circle forming and belief that it is occurring.

There are three important things within contemporary witchcraft as to why a circle is cast:

- **Creating a Sacred Space**: As the circle exists a "between the worlds", it is in effect liminal space where we can connect with the power and energy of our Gods, as well as any other beings or spirits that we wish to connect with. While we can actually do this anyway if we chose, when we create a specific place dedicated to those energies, it often enables us to have more effective communication.
- **Protection**: A well casted circle is able to keep unwanted spirits or entities out of your sacred space. It can help shield and protect you from negative energies or other influences.
- **Storing Energy**: Energy raised within a circle is contained there until it is raised. This enables cones of power to be created and directed towards particular goals. As such, when these are raised, the energy within a circle often becomes heavy and the temperature rises. Once the cone of power is released, the temperature tends to drop.

Exercise: Casting Your Circle

To physically cast a circle this requires "belief" in what you are doing as well as an understanding of what you are wishing to achieve. You will also need to know where the four directions are in the space that you are using. These can be found by using a compass (purchased from a camping store) or you might like to download a suitable app for your smartphone.

- Commence in the east, stand in a comfortable position,

ground and centre by following the Four-Fold Breath technique.

- Connect with the energy that flows throughout the universe by visualising (imagining) the energy through the top of your head and flowing through into your body. Hold your dominant hand out in front, pointing your ring and middle fingers, then slowly moving around to the north (south if you are in the Northern Hemisphere). As you move, visualise the energy projecting out through your fingertips and forming a circle behind you. This energy will also extend above and below you, encasing you in a sphere.
- Continue all around your space until you return to east again.
- Record in your magical diary how you felt about casting your first circle? Did you feel the energy or not?

If you did not feel anything, that is perfectly fine at this stage. The energies that we work with in the Craft tend to be rather subtle, so it could take a few goes before you begin to feel anything. The most important thing at this stage is for you to believe in what you are doing. Believe that you are casting a circle as opposed to merely walking around the room with your fingers pointed. The more you believe in what you are doing, the more you will feel the energies.

Exercise: Breathing in Cosmic Energy

- Sit in a comfortable seated position with your feet on the ground. Ground and centre by following the Four-Fold Breath technique.
- Focus on the vertical axis of your body. Allow yourself to find a comfortable position of balance where the vertical axis is calm, centred and effortless to maintain. Breathe slowly and deeply.
- Mentally reach out through the top of your head and

allow yourself to experience the infinite vastness of the sky and cosmos above you. Breathe into this vastness and imagine yourself drinking it in through the top of your head, pulling it down into your head, letting it cascade across your face, your ears, the back of your head, and down across your shoulders and arms.

- Allow your head to fill again with this "cosmic" energy, this time letting it tumble into your neck, down into your chest and filling your chest as you breathe in ... and out ... in and out. As the chest fills, let your stomach release, allowing the energy to fill your solar plexus, your abdomen, genital area, and down into your buttocks, through your legs, into your feet and out. Let it go deep into the earth. Repeat.

- Visualise your own internal structure as a spiral pathway to a small, bright light in the centre. Each time you inhale, the light spreads outwards a little more along the spiral pathway. Illumination grows with each breath, expelling the darkness. Soon the light will permeate your whole being. Imagine yourself afloat in light, partaking of the quality of light, becoming both the source and the essence of light.

- Visualise or imagine your inner self bathed in a pure white light, or if you prefer, in luminous rainbows of multi-coloured light. Allow yourself to become immersed in images of light. Let the light fill all parts of your spirit just as your blood fills all parts of your body, being direction by your heart, which is in turn connected to your breath.

- When you are ready, bring your awareness back to your physical body again, seated on the floor, your feet connected to the earth. With each breath, become more and more aware of the sounds around you, of your fingers and toes. Wriggle your fingers and toes, take a stretch and open your eyes.

- Record your experiences in your magical diary.

The more that you work with this exercise on a regular basis, the more comfortable you will become with it. So much so that you can begin working with the upward current in a similar manner. To do this, imagine the energy from the earth coming up through your feet and legs into your first chakra (*Muladhara*) which is located at the base of your spine, filling up there and flowing on into your genital area and abdomen, and solar plexus. It fills up again into your heart and chest, neck and shoulders, face and head, and out through the top of your head. This energy releases any tension it encounters outward and above. The objective is to work with this current until it flows smoothly.

Elemental Placements

Within contemporary witchcraft, the four elements, earth, air, fire and water, are called upon when erecting a magical circle as they are considered to be the building blocks of the universe (which will be discussed in more detail in the following section). Each element is usually assigned a specific direction depending on qualities.

Unless this is the first book you are reading on witchcraft and magick, I am sure that you would be familiar with the somewhat "standard" elemental placements of air in the east, fire in the south, water in the west, and earth in the north, which is fine if you reside in the Northern Hemisphere. However, as mentioned earlier, the elemental placements do tend to differ in the Southern Hemisphere, as well as for those people living closer to the equator. As such, discovering what is the most appropriate directions for each of the elements can be a bit daunting to a newcomer to contemporary witchcraft. This is why I have offered a simple exercise at the end of this section to encourage you to get out and observe your natural environment, as even the associations I use may not accurately work for you.

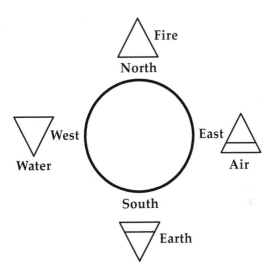

Elemental placement and directions with alchemical symbols
for the Southern Hemisphere

As I am based in South Australia, I use the following directions and elemental placements which is increasingly becoming a standard for the Southern Hemisphere:

- East = air: The sun rises in the east, similar to the Northern Hemisphere, and is the primary direction in most magical traditions. This the direction where I commence my circle-casting.
- North = fire: North of where I live is both the equator and the Simpson Desert. During summer the northerly winds are hot and dry blowing off the desert, and when the sun is at its zenith, it is in the north quarter of the sky. Therefore, it is appropriate that this direction is equated to the element of fire.
- West = water: West of Adelaide is the Spencer Gulf. This is the direction of the setting sun, and therefore water is the appropriate element to use.
- South = earth: South of where I live is Antarctica, the large

frozen continent. In winter, the southerly winds blow up from Antarctica and are cold. This is appropriate element to use is earth.

People living on the eastern seaboard of Australia, however, might use the following elemental directions, which reiterates why it is important to gain an understanding of your own local environment and ascertain for yourself the appropriate elemental directions:

- North = fire: This is similar to the above example as Australia is south of the equator.
- West = air: This direction is used because in Australia, winds blow across the continent from the Indian Ocean. However, some practitioners equate west with earth as to the west is the rest of continent.
- South = earth: Similar to the above example associated with the Antarctic and it is the traditional opposite of fire within a circle. (Some practitioners do equate the south with air).
- East = water: For the eastern states of Australia, the Pacific Ocean is to the east.

For followers of contemporary witchcraft who live on the west coast of Australia, west might be associated with water (the Indian Ocean) while east may be associated with earth (the rest of the Australia continent). These are just suggestions and at the end of the day, if the traditional Northern Hemispheric or Southern Hemispheric directions do not reflect your environment when feel free to change them. What is important is that you understand why you have placed the elements in the specific quarters around your circle.

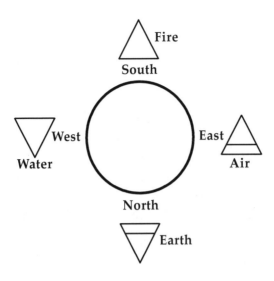

Elemental placement and directions with alchemical symbols
for the Northern Hemisphere

One part of my Craft is being in tune with my natural environment. As I have mentioned, contemporary witchcraft is about doing. You are not an observer. Learn the basics and form your foundation by following reputable instruction, however build your own house.

Exercise: Elemental Placements

- For this exercise, you need to venture out into your local environment three times a day and observe the movement of the sun. If you do not know where east is, you will need to obtain a compass (from a camping store) or download an appropriate app for your phone. Orientate yourself as to where the sun is upon rising or in the morning. Repeat at lunchtime or around 12 noon. Then repeat for a third time in the afternoon, prior to dusk. Internet sites such as Time and Date (https://www.timeanddate.com) can be used wherever you are located.

- Consider the above information about elemental placements around the circle. Record in your magical diary where you feel the elements are best placed for you, based on your own research and connection to your own environment.

You might also like to watch the nightly weather forecasts and take note of the direction and manner in which the weather patterns move across the country.

Some more traditional covens use the four winds when they cast their circles. I have personally ceased using these winds for many years now, largely because they tend to relate more to the Northern Hemisphere, i.e., being Greek in origin. Further, I simply do not believe that they relate or even resonate with the elemental directions and energies where I live south of the equator. This discussion has not always been received favourably by some more traditional witches. For me at the end of the day, that is what I consider to be more important. I am also sure that had the founders of my tradition been in a similar situation, they would have done what I have done – adapted their workings to their environmental energies. After all, contemporary witchcraft was said to be an ever-evolving tradition.

The Magical Altar

Creating a central point of focus can assist you in your meditation practice and within contemporary witchcraft. This usually comes in the form of an altar. Altars are used in many faiths. Their primary purpose is to give honour and reverence to the deity and to what we feel is sacred. The altar is also a place of sacrifice, of the transition or shifting of energy. It is also a place of manifestation on the inner planes. Just as the sacrifice or offering sends energy from this place of existence to another, the altar also serves as the focus when we bring through divine energy into this world (like a portal).

Within contemporary witchcraft, an altar serves three main purposes:

- Helps you centralise your personal energy and therefore each thing placed on it should have a specific purpose.
- For you to honour the Gods and your beliefs even when you are not physically present.
- Used as a work station in the creation of talismans, making herbal or healing potions, and so on.

There are usually no hard-and-fast rules as to what an altar should contain or be made of. It all depends on you – your taste and budget. A shelf, corner of your dressing table or an upside-down box is a good place to start. Traditionally, your altar should obtain objects that reflect what the God and Goddess mean to you. These could be statues, pictures, coloured candles or objects such as flowers, a pine-cone. Because your altar is your own personal space and place of worship, you should feel at ease to add whatever you wish to it.

Although traditional layout of the altar regards the left side as in honour of the Goddess, the right as in honour of the God, and the centre for spirit, it is not necessary that you feel obligated to follow this layout. Other traditions recommend that the four elements (air, water, fire and earth) be represented and their attributing tools should be placed that direction. For example, a feather, wand, incense burner etc representing air should be placed in the east; a chalice, cup, sea shell representing water should be placed in the west, and so on. Again, this is a personal choice. I suggest to my students that they spend time arranging their altar so that it is both pleasing as well as practical. Most importantly, your altar should represent your own form and style of honouring and connection with the Gods.

Tools that are used within contemporary witchcraft are discussed in a later chapter. For now, however, the single

• process of constructing a central focus is all that you need to concern yourself with. Be mindful if you share your living arrangements with other people, as they might not be all that open to you outwardly expressing your newly-found spiritual belief. In such situations, you might prefer to set up your altar in your bedroom, e.g., on a bookshelf or on top of your dressing table. The altar may only consist of a candle (tee lights are fine) and a few crystals and images that reflect the elements and the Gods to you.

Placement of the altar itself is also considered within contemporary witchcraft. It is common for an altar to be placed in one of three main directions:

- **The Dark Quarter**: This refers to the direction where the "sun never shines", which is a magical concept as opposed to a physical one. In other words, you may view it as this: the sun rises in the east, sets in the west, and is at its zenith either in the south in the Northern Hemisphere or the north in the Southern Hemisphere. Therefore, the "dark quarter" is the north in the Northern Hemisphere and the south in the Southern Hemisphere.
- **East**: This is the direction of the rising sun and where all things begin – a favoured direction for those following ceremonial and Egyptian magick.
- **Centre**: In this direction it is easy to face any direction. The centre of your magical circle, again, is a direction probably more associated with ceremonial magick as opposed to contemporary witchcraft.

Whatever direction your altar faces, make sure you understand the energies of that particular element and the meanings that it hold. It is also recommended that you use a compass to find out where the directions are. Should your altar be part of a bookcase, or your room is designed where your altar cannot face the appropriate direction, then make do with what you have.

If your altar does not face the preferred direction all this means is that when you cast your circle you will have to move to that direction. Also be mindful of the energies of that direction that your altar is facing, especially if you are using it as a focal point for empowerment rituals and spells, etc.

Exercise: Creating Your Sanctuary

- Sit in a comfortable seated position with your feet on the ground. Ground and centre by following the Four-Fold Breath technique.
- Visualise that you are in some beautiful, natural environment such as in a meadow, a forest, or even beside the sea. Wherever it is, it should be comfortable, pleasant and peaceful for you.
- Begin to explore your environment. Take notice of what you see, the sounds around you and any smells. Also take note of any particular feelings or impressions you get.
- Begin to add anything to your sanctuary that will make it more homelike and comfortable for you. You might want to build some type of house or shelter, or perhaps just surround the whole area with a golden light of protection and safety. Create and arrange things there for your convenience and enjoyment, or do a ritual to establish it as your special personal sanctuary.
- When you are ready to come back, slowly begin to move your fingers and toes. Then open your eyes when you feel ready to come back to normal consciousness.
- Remember to record any feelings, visions or problems you have in your magical diary.

From now on, this is your own personal sanctuary to which you can return at any time, just by closing your eyes and desiring to be there. You will also find it healing and relaxing to be there. It is a place of special power for you, and you may wish to go there every time you do visualisation.

You can make changes and additions to it any time, but just remember to retain the primary qualities of peacefulness and a feeling of absolute safety.

A final word on altars. In this age of social media, it is common for newcomers to Wicca to share or ask to share photos of their altars. If you are wishing to embrace contemporary witchcraft as your path then I suggest you consider what I have previously mentioned about one of the main roles or aspects of an altar is that it is a personal "reservoir" of your own energy. This reservoir increases and deepens in potency the more you utilise it. As such, I personally would not recommend sharing images of your altar, ritual workings or spell craftings because in doing so, what you effectively are doing is actually lessening your energy reservoir, and even diminishing the successfulness of any ritual or spell that you are crafting.

If you must share a photo, I would recommend that you strip it down to the bare bones or even decorate the altar in a way that does not actually reflect your ongoing work. For example, I may share images of my altar setup prior to the commencement of the actual ritual and before I have actually finalised the placement of all the objects. Or I may share a photo of after the event where items have been removed.

The Elements and the Elementals

In contemporary witchcraft, everything can be related back to the four elements: earth, air, fire and water. The ritual tools we use, astrological signs, aspects of nature, and even aspects of our personality. This is why a considerable amount of time is given to learning about the elements, their rhythms in nature and within our own selves. In fact, some say that the secrets of the universe are all contained within the elements.

The elements are considered to be the four building blocks of everything that has physical existence within the universe. They represent the world in which we live, their own elemental worlds (or realms), and have various magical associations. No element exists in a pure form as we know it: Fire needs fuel (earth) and oxygen (air) to burn. There is air within water otherwise seaweed and fish would die. Even the earth is filled with air and water. These elements show us the interconnectedness of all things, for "As above, so below", i.e., the universe (or macrocosm) and us (or microcosm).

Spirit, the fifth element, binds the physical to the astral or the spiritual. It is consciousness, the soul, chi, prana, etc, permeating all things in differing degrees and ways, i.e., the healing energies travelling through the hands of a Reiki healer is spirit.

In my tradition of contemporary witchcraft, knowing and understanding the elements is essential. This is because everything comes back to them. In the Outer Court training that I teach, neophytes are expected to establish an intimate relationship with each element. After all, this is of assistance when the elements are called into the magical circle.

Air: Related to both fire (active) and water (passive), has the dryness of fire and the humidity of water. Is very balanced, soft, gentle and fluid, yet capable of transmitting tremendous force. Air is the element of thought, mind, the intangibles, which we know exist but cannot prove. Air is the breath that we take in. Air is with us every day of our lives, from birth until death. Air rules psychic abilities, especially telepathy and divination or prophecy. Earth is an air purifier, and clean air supports life. We begin  to understand the inter-connectedness of things. Air takes the stability of earth and sends it soaring.

- Direction: East
- Colour: Yellow
- Magical Tool: Wand
- Other Associations: Bell, incense, censer, feather, music, poetry, birds, butterflies
- Elemental Being: Sylphs
- Other Beings: Faeries, clouds
- Hour of day: Dawn
- Season: Spring
- Hermetic Axiom: To Know
- Aspect: Passive masculine
- Zodiacal signs: Gemini, Libra, Aquarius
- Representations: Breath, wind, sound, speech, communication, thought, image
- Crystals: Clear quartz, blue lace agate, turquoise, chrysocolla
- Sense: Smell
- Body: Mind, speech, intuition, mental ability
- Qualities (Positive): Inspiration, wisdom, happiness, hope, logic, joy, analysis, discernment, decisiveness
- Qualities (Negative): Anxiety, fear, impulsiveness, paranoia, dispersion prejudice, insecurity

Exercise: Air Elemental Pore Breathing
- Sit in a comfortable seated position with your feet on the

ground. Ground and centre by following the Four-Fold Breath technique.

- Imagine yourself to be in the middle of a mass of air that is filling the whole universe. Nothing exists around you except for the air-filled space embracing the whole universe. Inhale the air element into your empty vessel of the soul, every breath filling the whole body with more air. Continue for five minutes.
- Imagine yourself resembling a balloon becoming lighter and lighter each time you inhale. Continue until you do not feel your body at all. Continue for a further five minutes.
- Reverse the process. As you exhale, breath the element back out into the universe again, exhaling an equivalent number as inhalations, until you are complete.

Fire: Heat and expansion. In its active mode, fire is potent, violent, and destructive. In its passive mode it is peaceful, warm, sustaining, illuminating – it is very much a double-edged sword. It is the element of power, strength, determination, courage, change, will and  passion. It is all energy, creativity and sensuality, as well as the spark of divinity which shines within us and all living things. It is at once the most physical and spiritual of all the elements.

- Direction: North (Southern Hemisphere) or South (Northern Hemisphere)
- Colour: Red
- Magical Tool: Athame
- Other Associations: Candles, lamps, volcanic rock
- Elemental Being: Salamanders
- Other Beings: Fire Faeries
- Hour of day: Noon

- Season: Summer
- Hermetic Axiom: To Will
- Aspect: Active masculine
- Zodiacal signs: Aries, Leo, Sagittarius
- Representations: Energy, movement, will, power, passion, electricity, action, interaction, growth
- Crystals: Carnelian, tiger's eye, ruby, garnet
- Sense: Sight
- Body: Digestive system, circulatory system
- Qualities (Positive): Courage, motivation, drive, enthusiasm, passion, will
- Qualities (Negative): Fickleness, vengefulness, violence, possessiveness, hatred, cruelty, egotism

Exercise: Fire Elemental Pore Breathing
(If you have high blood-pressure do not attempt this exercise)
-
- Sit in a comfortable seated position with your feet on the ground. Ground and centre by following the Four-Fold Breath technique.
- Imagine yourself in the centre of the fiery element which, as a ball shape, envelops the universe. All around you is fiery. Inhale the fire element with your nose, drawing in deep breaths. Your physical and astral bodies resemble empty vessels into which the element is being inhaled or sucked in with each breath. Continue for five minutes.
- This heat grows more and more intense with every breath. Its expansion power becomes stronger and the fiery pressure higher, until you feel yourself fiery red hot.
- Reverse the process. As you exhale, breathe the element back out into the universe again, exhaling an equivalent number as inhalations, until you are complete.

Water: Fluidity, harmony, and passivity. Water is the ultimate catalytic force, without which life as we know it could not exist. It flows to seek the lowest level of any surface, controlling nothing, but seeking harmony with its surroundings and yet, given time, it can dissolve almost anything and no force can compress it.

Water is associated with memory, ancestor, and past lives. It is the element of emotions, as most of our memories are triggered by how we feel or felt about them. In its active mode, water is energetic and powerful, but can be very destructive (tidal waves, tsunamis, floods and hurricanes). In its passive mode (lakes, streams, rain) it is life-giving, nourishing and protective.

- Direction: West
- Colour: Blue
- Magical Tool: Chalice
- Other Associations: Cup, water, blood/wine, shells, coral, ocean stones
- Elemental Being: Undines
- Other Beings: Mermaids, Sea nymphs
- Hour of day: Afternoon
- Season: Autumn
- Hermetic Axiom: To Dare
- Aspect: Passive feminine
- Zodiacal signs: Cancer, Scorpio, Pisces
- Representations: Emotions, dreams, intuition, unconsciousness, blood, flow
- Crystals: Opal, blue quartz, pearls
- Sense: Taste
- Body: Urinary system
- Qualities (Positive): Compassions, sympathy, empathy, nurture, sexuality, trust, serenity, tranquillity, depth
- Qualities (Negative): Jealousy, hatred, insipid, treachery, sorrow, deceit, spite, venom

Exercise: Water Elemental Pore Breathing

- Sit in a comfortable seated position with your feet on the ground. Ground and centre by following the Four-Fold Breath technique.
- Imagine the whole universe is an enormous ocean and you are in the centre of it. Your body becomes filled with this element with each whole-body breath. Feel the cold of the water in your whole body with each breath you take. Continue for five minutes.
- Reverse the process. As you exhale, breath the element back out into the universe again, exhaling an equivalent number as inhalations, until you are complete.

Earth: Is related to the other three elements, as it involves all of them in a solid form. The properties of the element earth are heaviness, solidity, and closeness. Earth is a very passive element, teaching strength, resolution, steadfastness, integrity. It brings harmony, 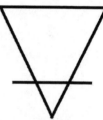 cyclical growth and replenishment. Yet earth has its active side – earthquakes, avalanches, rock falls – in which the earth's awesome and usually silent force speaks and speaks loudly. The Greeks considered earth to be a symbol of the physical state of being that we call "solid". It is a handful of soil from the garden, it is the entire planet. Earth does not necessary represent the physical earth, but that part of it which is stable, solid and dependable.

- Direction: South (Southern Hemisphere) or North (Northern Hemisphere)
- Colour: Green
- Magical Tool: Pentacle
- Other Associations: Soil, plants, coins, stones, bones, pine cones

- Elemental Being: Gnomes
- Other Beings: Wood nymphs, dryads, trolls, elves
- Hour of day: Midnight
- Season: Winter
- Hermetic Axiom: To Keep Silent
- Aspect: Active feminine
- Zodiacal signs: Taurus, Virgo, Capricorn
- Representations: The physical body, endurance, the planet, substance, manifestation, results, matter, practicalities
- Crystals: Smoky quartz, obsidian, onyx, moss agate, jade, green aventurine
- Sense: Touch
- Body: The skeleton
- Qualities (Positive): Strength, stability, humility, selflessness, patience, responsibility, persistence, tolerance
- Qualities (Negative): Laziness, stubbornness, greed, attention seeking, inertia, domineering, depression, melancholy

Exercise: Earth Elemental Pore Breathing

- Sit in a comfortable seated position with your feet on the ground. Ground and centre by following the Four-Fold Breath technique.
- Imagine the whole universe being the earth – dense material with yourself sitting in the middle of it. The specific property of this earthy material is density and gravity. Fill your body with this heavy material. With each inhalation, your body is getting heavier and heavier, until it begins to resemble a lump of lead. Continue for five minutes.
- Reverse the process. As you exhale, breath the element back out into the universe again, exhaling an equivalent number as inhalations, until you are complete.

Spirit: The animating force, everywhere present, and everywhere abundant. It is energy and the eternal in essence.

- Direction: Centre
- Colour: White
- Magical Tool: The Circle
- Other Associations: God and Goddess images, paintings, crystals, prayers, mantras, mandalas, music
- Elemental Being: The Gods
- Other Beings: Devas, fairies, spirits, ghosts
- Hour of day: Between the Worlds
- Season: The Wheel of the Year
- Represents: Source, psyche, soul, outer space, infinity, cosmic intelligence, psychic energy, deity consciousness
- Crystals: Clear quartz, amethyst, sodalite
- Sense: Hearing
- Qualities (Positive): Will, harmony, transformation
- Qualities (Negative): There are none.

The Elementals

These beings are best described as spirits or entities of the elemental realms. They are believed to be primitive, non-human and non-material entities of the nature belonging to one of the four elements. If you have ever been transfixed with fascination watching a building or forest burn; or when standing on a high balcony or an exposed cliff face, had an unaccountable urge to throw yourself from it; then you have experienced something of the power of the elementals.

Everything on our physical plane is made up of a combination of the elements, but elementals are totally composed of only one element. It is because of this that they are rarely seen on this plane except within their own element. Salamanders are sometimes seen around roaring fires and sylphs are sometimes seen as sparkles in the air on a clear day.

Each elemental is associated with a different element:

- Elemental spirits of earth are called gnomes and their ruler is Gnob.
- Elemental spirits of air are called sylphs (similar to faeries), and their ruler is Paralda.
- Elemental spirits of water are called undines (similar to mermaids and mermen), and their ruler is Niksa.
- Elemental spirits of fire are called salamanders (similar to the fire lizards), and their ruler is Djinn.

British occultist Dion Fortune talks about contact with the elementals as follows:

"Any elemental contact is stimulating to us, because elemental beings pour forth in abundance the vitality of their own particular sphere, and this vitalizes the corresponding element in ourselves. But if a four-element creature is drawn into the sphere of a single element, he is poisoned by an overdose of the one element in which he finds himself, and starved of the other three. It is for this reason that mortals in the fairy kingdom are always said to be enchanted or asleep."[44]

Elementals are powerful, unpredictable and can be dangerous if you do not understand their natural realms nor know how to banish them correctly.

Magical Working Tools

When Gerald Gardner founded contemporary witchcraft, he incorporated into its structure a number of Masonic teachings through his own influences. In Freemasonry the tools, in particular the chalice (cup), the pentacle, the athame and the wand, all have specific meanings, not only relating to each of the four elements, but also deeper more personal meanings which are only usually realised upon dedication and initiation and its related progression down the particular path. These meanings have been carried through into contemporary witchcraft.

Within contemporary witchcraft, when the neophyte is training for their first degree initiation, they are expected to work with and understand the elements. At their initiation, they are presented with the four main tools whose meanings are disclosed. It is then up to the newly initiated witch to meditate on the tools to discover, if you like, the hidden keys and doors that each key will unlock. This is part of the mysteries that are contained within contemporary witchcraft.

According to Gardner, when a person is initiated into contemporary witchcraft as a first degree, they are expected to either create or purchase their own set of ritual tools. One of the requirements for the second degree initiation is not only being able to name all of the ritual tools, but also to explain what their purpose and associations are within the tradition. Today solitaries tend to have their own set of tools even if they are not initiated or properly prepared (as Gardner once instructed.)

From the get go the neophyte of contemporary witchcraft is introduced to the tools that are used within the Craft and are encouraged to commence cultivating a relationship with them. In my tradition the athame (what Gardner referred to as "the true witch's weapon") is aligned with the element of fire (after all metal is forged in fire, and the athame is also more direct than the wand), however other traditions associate the athame with air (following the teachings of ceremonial magick). Therefore, depending on the tradition of contemporary witchcraft the neophyte is being trained in, this will depend on the teaching they receive about each of the tools, coupled with their own personal gnosis about the energy of that tool, together with how it relates to their craft.

As a rule of thumb, the four main tools are:

- The **athame**, traditionally is black handled, with a double-edged blade. It is used to direct energy for the casting of magick circles, controlling of spirits and other ritual purposes. In my tradition the athame cuts a doorway between this physical realm and the other realms (i.e., that of spirit) enabling the witch to step "between the worlds". As such, the athame relates to the element of fire, however it is also associated with air in other traditions.

- The **wand** is, according to Gardener, "used to summon certain spirits with whom it would not be meet to use the athame". Therefore, the wand is a tool of invocation, used to evoke the Gods, and to channel energy as a means of invitation as opposed to commanding. It is also used in healing rituals, spell-casting, and rites such as "Drawing Down the Moon". As such, the wand relates to the element of air (or fire depending on tradition).

- The **chalice** is symbolic of the Goddess, particularly her sacred womb from which we are all born from. It connects the witch to the subliminal dreamlike realms and therefore relates to the element of water.

- The **pentacle** is a disk often engraved or containing the five-pointed star, the pentagram. It is believed to magically energizes anything that is placed upon it. It also connects the witch with to power of the land as well as the realm of the ancestors. As such the pentacle relates to the element of earth.

When the neophyte forges a relationship with each of their tools, they also forge a relationship with each of the four elements. As I have already mentioned, within my tradition of contemporary witchcraft this relationship with each of the four elements is vitally important. The fifth element, that being spirit, can be perceived almost as the overseeing element, or even the completed result. A more detailed look at each of the four main tools as they appear in relationship to the elemental directions of the magick circle:

- **Wand**: The wand is traditionally measured from inside the elbow to the tip of the middle finger. Representing the full extension of the arm, this measurement also represents the full extension of one's personal power in the world. Woods that are commonly used include oak, willow and ash. I made my first wand however, from a branch from a fruit tree that broke during a storm.

  Within the magick circle, the wand is used to channel power and is considered to be a tool of persuasion. It can also be used to summon energies where the use of an athame would be inappropriate. The wand is a masculine tool and can be associated with the element of fire within some traditions. Within my tradition of contemporary witchcraft, it represents the element of air, the element that rules the mind and communication.

  Of all the magical tools, the wand is probably the easiest to make yourself, using a branch as I did or even a piece of dowel obtained from a hardware store. Some people decorate their wands with crystals and copper wire (believed to have the ability to conduct spiritual energy back and forth between people, crystals, auras, the mind and the spirit world), others leave their wands plain. There are really no hard or fast rules save that you should be guided by what appeals to you.

- **Athame**: The primary tool in contemporary witchcraft is the athame, traditionally a double-bladed knife with a black hilt. Each side of the blade is said to represent the God and the Goddess respectfully, coming together at a point that further represents the union of the mundane and the magical realms. This balance of polarities can be seemed as a Craft version of the Eastern yin and yang. As mentioned earlier while some traditions the athame is associated with the element of air, in my tradition of contemporary witchcraft it is associated with fire, representing inspiration and passion. This is because as the metal is forged in fire, that athame is believed to retain the memory of this transformative power.

  To employ the athame is to declare possession of the power to magically transform something. The athame communicates the message that "I can reshape you, transform you, and carve you anew", making it a tool of command. In ritual, the athame is used for casting or banishing circles. It can also be used to evoke the Watchtowers by the drawing of associated pentagrams, which are then opened as portals. It should never be used for cutting or drawing blood.

  When enacting the symbolic Great Rite, the athame represents the masculine aspect.

  Of all the magical tools, the athame is probably the more difficult to obtain, at least within Australia due to the various State knife laws, and is probably one of the more expensive tools if you wish to purchase a proper one (that being one with a double-edged blade). Despite this, most contemporary witchcraft covens do insist that initiates should own their own athame. I purchased my first athame back in the 1990s while overseas prior to any knife laws. I was later gifted another blade by an Australian blacksmith. The athame I use within my teaching circles was also gifted from a past student prior to them moving interstate.

- **Chalice** or **Cup**: The chalice or cup is used to hold the ritual wine that is blessed at the end of the ritual. Water used to consecrate the ritual space can be contained in a second chalice or bowl. While in contemporary witchcraft the chalice can be made out of any substance, such as glass, pottery, pewter, or even wood; in ceremonial magick, however, blue glass is preferred. Within a spiritual context, the chalice is a vessel of offering and receptivity. Just as we, as worshippers of deity, are in effect vessels awaiting the pouring forth of spiritual light, so too is the chalice the vessel of containment and fulfilment.

  The chalice holds the intimate liquids of ritual celebration, just as we ourselves are filled with red liquid essence/blood. In this concept we find affinity with the chalice, and in the relationship of being filled and emptied in our own existence. The chalice is not so much a tool representative of the element of which it is made. The power of the chalice lies more in polarity, what it can contain rather than what concept its material connects it to.

  When enacting the symbolic Great Rite, the chalice represents the feminine aspect and is associated with element of water.

  I have a number of chalices, most are coloured glass obtained from second hand stores or markets, including a green one with oak leaves that is used during sabbats. I also have a pewter and glass chalice that I use for full moon esbats.

- **Pentacle**: Sometimes called pantacle, this is a flat disk which is commonly made from copper, brass or wood inscribed with a pentagram (five-pointed star which represents the four elements and spirit). Other symbols representing various initiated degrees, the God and Goddess, astrological signs and the like, can also be inscribed upon the pentacle. Circular wooden bases can be obtained from hardware or craft stores. Alternatively, you may like to make one yourself out of clay. In the British Museum there are examples of pentacles that English magician John Dee used that are made from wax.

The pentacle is a symbol of protection and as such is the centre point of the altar upon which items that are to be consecrated are placed.

In the magical sense, the five-pointed star etched upon the pentacle symbolises the principle of elemental harmony bound to the physical dimension. To brandish the pentacle is to wield the power to evoke balance and harmony, to bind chaos. It can also be used to keep negative energies out of the circle during your rituals, as well as providing the power to command and control the forces. To astral spirits, thoughts are actual things, and therefore presenting the pentacle to them evokes the principle it represents, making it a reality to which they must comply.

The pentacle is a feminine tool and represents the element of earth.

My own pentacle was purchased from an occult specialist store when I was living in England in the 1990s and follows a more traditional design with appropriate symbols. You can make your own pentacle from wooden rounds purchased from hardware stores that are then painted and varnished. Alternatively you can use a ceramic tile and paint a pentagram inside a circle on it.

Other Working Tools

There are various other tools that are used within contemporary witchcraft. The more common ones are:

- **Bell**: A bell, or gong, can be used at the commencement of the rituals to announce the commencement of a ritual or magical working. It is also used to cleanse the ritual space.
- **Besom**: The witch's broom. Traditionally, it was used during fertility rites. In ritual, the besom is used to sweep away negative energy to cleanse and purify your working area. It can also be used as an instrument of protection if hung or placed by the front or back door of the home.
- **Boline**: A single-edged, white-handled knife used to cut, carve or inscribe things in the course of a ritual. Sometimes it resembles a miniature sickle. It is also used when harvesting herbs.
- **Cauldron**: From the brewing of potions and herbal remedies, though to simply the cooking pot, the cauldron is a feminine symbol and is often associated with the womb of the Goddess. It can contain the ritual fire, and can also be used as a scrying tool.
- **Cords**: Depending on tradition, cords have a number of different uses. They are used for binding the seeker in initiation rites, denoting differing degrees of attainment, magick, or simply as a piece of apparel circling the waist.
- **Scourge**: This tool is often associated more with Gardnerian witchcraft. The scourge has two main functions - the first is purely symbolic, and the second is for gentle, monotonous, semi-hypnotic application to affect the blood circulation as an aid to gaining second sight. Used more within groups.
- **Skull**: While more commonly found within traditional non-Gardnerian influenced witchcraft, skulls can also be used within contemporary witchcraft where they represent the Watchtowers or the Dread Lord of the Outer

Space who are believed to escort the souls of the deceased into the other realms. Such a belief is believed to have stemmed from earlier Greek philosophers who considered that the increasing light of the waxing moon was due to the gathering of souls of the dead. The skull therefore connects us to our ancestors.

• **Stang**: In traditional non-Gardnerian influenced witchcraft, stangs guard the entrance into the ritual circle. They also can be decorated to represent the God with a candle placed "between the horns" and beneath would be a mask, garlands or cross arrows depending on tradition.

Each of the tools is as much a part of the energy of deity, the God and Goddess, as we are and as such, they enable us to align with our intention in greater strength and stability than if we were to attempt it alone. However, it only truly occurs when an intimate relationship with that specific tool has been established. If there is no relationship present between the witch and their athame for example, then the athame is merely just a physical object and while it may still be a manifestation of divine energy, the vibrational frequency of that object will be inaccessible to the witch.

The tools that each witch owns hold a personality. They are a living energy that is available for the witch to utilize. For example, every athame will feel energetically different, just as every wand, every chalice, and pentacle. For this reason, it is considered inappropriate to touch another witch's tools, especially once they are consecrated because of the direct energy connection with its owner.

Insight into the Pentagram

Not to be confused with a pentacle, the pentagram is a five pointed star that has been used almost since the dawn of time for various reasons, more commonly as a representation of the concept of the "human being made perfect" incorporating the four elements (earth, fire, water and air) with spirit, the element that links us to the divine. Leonardo da Vinci's sketch of the "Vitruvian Man" highlights this connection of man with the elements, and as such, stresses the belief that the flow of the entire universe requires a harmony in these elements, from the most cosmic macrocosm to the tiniest microcosm.

Each of the points of the pentagram relates to a particular element and correspondence. This relation is believed to stem back to ancient times. Within my own tradition, there is a connection to the deeper mysteries that cannot be explained in depth here save for the use of the human body in connection to each of the elemental placements:

- **Spirit** (head): This element relates to our connection to the Gods, the divine, our own holy guardian angel. Spirit also relates to the fact the contemporary witchcraft is a Mystery tradition into which the neophyte ultimately desires to be initiated into.
- **Air** (left hand): This element relates to the mind, intellect, word, thoughts, philosophy, our ideas about the universe and our world view.
- **Earth** (left foot): This element relates to our connection with the earth, the physical realm. It also relates to the practical application of the knowledge that we learn.
- **Fire** (right foot): This element relates to our will, passion and the magical powers contained within the teachings of contemporary witchcraft.
- **Water** (right hand): This element relates to our emotions, the love which unites and binds us to other people as well as the universe around us.

Within contemporary witchcraft there are eight variations of the pentagram that are used, two of each relating to each element, one to invoke the elemental energy while the other to banish. Examples of these pentagrams can be found in the Appendix. The pentagram that most people are familiar with is the "banishing pentagram of earth" which is often used on its own as a form of protection.

When the pentagram is inverted or reversed (upside down), this generally is interpreted as the four elements ruling over spirit, or a connection with the physical realm. While such a symbol is commonly associated with Satanism and the Left-Hand Path these days (where the two upward points represent the horns of the devil), this is not the only association. Within contemporary witchcraft the inverted pentagram can reflect a symbol for the Horned God, or a person who has obtained the rank of Second Degree.

Obsession with Crystals

In recent years there seems to be an obsession with crystals. Save for an obsidian scrying mirror or ball, very few crystals are actually traditionally used within contemporary witchcraft. These days modern Wiccans tend to have an abundance of crystals if the photos posted on social media are anything to go by.

Personally, I like crystals – after all I make devotional beads and bracelets from them. I tend to use them in my energetic healing practices. Some may even find their way into my spell workings however they do not necessary form a major part of my craft. Having said this, I do have some pieces of quartz in my garden around my magical circle – however these are natural pieces of quartz from my local environment and are used to help grounding energy raised.

What is Ritual?

The *Oxford Dictionary* describes "ritual" as "a ceremonial act or series of acts, a prescribed method of procedure". The use of ritual in religion and magick has been around for thousands of years. Our ancient Palaeolithic ancestors had specialised rituals, particular around the burial of the dead. Graves have been discovered when the deceased was laid to rest with their hunting tools, items of spiritual or magical significance, and bowls of food in preparation of their journey to the Otherworld. Images have also decorated caves of rituals enacted out to aid the hunt and of celebration. In some parts of the world today some of these ancient rituals are still being performed.

Within magical circles, a ritual is described as being "an act of worship or magick that employs a specific series of stages using symbolism and ceremony to create a sacred space and state of consciousness whereby participants are put in touch with forces outside themselves (i.e., the Gods)."[45] Therefore, when we perform any kind of ritual, it is important to remember that what we are going is creating a link and cultivating a dialogue between the microcosm (our "little world") and the macrocosm (the "great world").

In order for us to work ritual effectively, we need to:

- Fully understand what we are doing and why we are doing it (ritual intent).
- Be properly prepared, purified and consecrated (mind, body and soul).
- Have a firm understanding of the magical language being used (symbolism and myth).
- Be able to fully concentrate on the goal.
- Relinquish our ego in order to work within the group consciousness.

Rituals also form part of our everyday lives as we act in a certain way to achieve a particular goal. From the moment we awaken and make ourselves ready for the day ahead, to the time we prepared ourselves for sleep, we are performing rituals. In magick, ritual can be perceived as a tool which can be used to focus the mind and energies. Although there are many differing types of magical rites and rituals, they all have their own specific and predetermined purpose. Within contemporary witchcraft there are three main categories into which rituals fall:

- To mark a specific occasion such as a sabbat (dates that mark the changing of the seasons as well as the solstices and equinoxes) or an esbat (rituals held on or around the full moon),
- For the creation of a specific magical act, such as healing, or acquiring material wealth, or
- For spiritual enlightenment, achieving information and knowledge from the higher realms, to become one with your higher self, you own Godhead or Higher Guardian Angel, or even guidance and direction when faced with a decision.

When we create ritual and weave our magick, our goal is more than just the here and now. What we are intending to do is to tap into the egregore, the conscious mind, of those who have been creating ritual and weaving magick before us. This is especially so when initiated into a tradition. As such, what we are effectively doing with each magical rite we perform is adding our energy to what has gone before.

As you prepare your candles, incense, the placement of tools upon the altar, and so on, you have begun to condition and programme yourself to the concepts of eternal truth and wisdom. They are already there, but you had begun to release them when you made the preparation for the magick circle – the meeting place between the worlds of the Gods and of men.

The circle is a focus of earth energy as well as a symbolic representation on earth of the motion of the cosmos above us. Like all magick, a combination of the cosmos and the earth – as above, so below. For when we cast, or visualise, a circle, we are attempting to create a microcosm which contains all that is found in the macrocosm. Therefore, we ensure that we follow the energies of our physical location; we also ensure that we follow, as our ancestors did when they constructed the stone circles, the motions of the cosmos.

Basic Ritual Etiquette

The circle that you cast is not an imaginary construct, although it may seem like it is just a figment of your imagination when you first begin. When you believe in what you doing, and have 100% faith in your Craft, then this makes your magick more effective. This is done through respecting the energies that you are working with, even if you do not completely understand how they work at the time. As such, the following are a few guidelines that will further enhance the power and energy in your circle:

- Ensure that you will not be disturbed. Turn your mobile phone off or better still, leave it outside your sacred space.
- Make sure that your ritual robe or attire is clean.
- You are "properly prepared", i.e., that you are in the right frame of mind.
- When you move around in your circle do so in a deosil direction (anti-clockwise in the Southern Hemisphere or clockwise in the Northern Hemisphere). By moving in a deosil circle you connect with the energies that you are raising as well as the circle itself. This is discussed further when I discuss about raising a "Cone of Power".
- If you have undertaken a ritual in nature, ensure that you tidy up after yourself. My initial instructions were to leave

the space I was using cleaner than how I found it. In other words, picking up any rubbish that other people may have left behind.

- Ensure that you dispose of items appropriately, i.e., incense, candles, any petitions or spells that need to be "dissolved" by nature.

Preparing Yourself for Ritual

In some traditions, particularly those which are inspired by Egyptian sources, when we create a ritual space, we are in fact creating the "holy of holies" into which we invite the Gods to attend. As such not only should be this place be cleansed, but also so should we be.

As I am fortunate to have a separate room set aside for my rituals, the first thing I do is to ensure that the altar is set up appropriately and then to physically sweep or vacuum the area in a deosil direction. As mentioned previously, ritual does not begin when you cast your circle, ritual actually begins when you decide to create a ritual. Some people like to smudge their ritual area and use incenses or room sprays such as white sage, palo santo, or frankincense. Once the ritual space is set up, I then cleanse myself.

Depending on what I have been doing prior to ritual, how I feel, or what the ritual is for, I may physically wash myself by having a shower using a special salt scrub that I keep especially for this purpose. (See Appendix for a recipe to make your own salt scrub.) Alternatively, I at least wash my face, hands and feet before entering my ritual space. Another way of cleansing your ritual space and even yourself is through the use of sound. You might like to use a bell, rattle, singing bowl or even a drum to dissipate any stagnant or negative energies.

I then spend some time in meditation, or at least quiet contemplation, calming my mind, relaxing my physical body and through performing techniques such as the Four-Fold Breath, begin to get into "ritual consciousness" and opening myself up to working magick and being in communication with the Gods.

Ritual Structure

The structure of performing a rite or ritual will differ greatly on the need of the individual, as well as how they work. Some rites and ritual follow a formalised structure which I term as the "Eight Points of Ritual Work". These are:

1. **Preparation**: The gathering of all the information and ingredients or tools you need for a specific working.

2. **Purification**: Setting up the area you will be using by constructing an altar, cleansing the area with incense and salted water. Making yourself ready by either with a ritual bath and/or a brief meditation about what it is you are about to undertake.

3. **Physical Circle Casting**: This can be either visualising yourself in a bubble of protection, or physically casting a circle around the space you are to work in, usually done in a deosil (anti-clockwise in the Southern Hemisphere or clockwise in the Northern Hemisphere) direction. There are a number of differing methods to do this depending on what beliefs you have and what tradition you are following. After the circle is physically casted, the elemental representations are then taken around the circle, commencing with incense (element of air), a candle (fire) and a mixture of salt (earth) and water (water). When the salt water is taken around, it is asperged, i.e., sprinkled or flicked.

4. **Invocation of the Elemental Quarters**: Calling upon the elemental guardians of each quarter to protect your circle.

5. **Invocation of Deity**: Calling upon the Gods or a specific deity who you have chosen to work with to attend your circle and witness what you are doing.

6. **Main Body of the Ritual**: This may include crafting a spell and then raising energy to direct towards the empowerment of that particular spell, meditating on an issue, or communing with the Gods. Within contemporary witchcraft the energy raised is called a "Cone of Power" and is usually one of the first things that occurs after the Gods have been evoked.

7. **Libation**: The sharing of wine or juice and cakes or bread with the Gods is a common practical found within contemporary witchcraft, especially at sabbats (seasonal rituals) or esbats (full moons) where libations and offerings are made.

8. **Banishing the Circle**: Acknowledging and thanking the Gods that you have asked to aid you, thanking and dismissing the elemental guardians. Banishing your circle that you have constructed on the astral and declare that your ritual has completed. Then packing away the things that you have used (if need be, extinguishing candles (or putting them in a safe place to burn out), and so on.

Additional steps can also be added depending on the path you are following, or the type of rite or ritual you are performing. However, due to the simplistic nature of magick, formalised ritual work is not always necessary. For example, the simple decision of carrying a certain crystal with you is a form of magick as you are opening yourself up to the powers of that crystal.

If you are new to ritual work, the best place to start is by deciding what you want to create a ritual for:

- Do you wish to attune yourself to the natural energies of the earth and celebrate the coming sabbat or esbat?
- Do you have a particular desire or goal you wish to achieve?
- Is there something in your life you would like some insight

into?

• Do you want to craft a spell, or make a magical item?

When you have decided on the purpose, the next step is to find somewhere suitable in which to hold your ritual.

As the energies worked with in magick are very subtle, the way they affect us, or the result of any ritual performed, will not be seen immediately. This is why, as mentioned earlier, I recommend that all my students record their workings in a diary of some kind, as this is the best way to notice the changes as they happen. The changes can also affect you in ways not anticipated, such as how you perceive the world, and even those around you. Even if you are not performing rituals or crafting spells, you start to make small observations that you never noticed before. The simple delight in seeing the first buds on a tree indicating that spring is on its way, the subtle way the lunar energies affect you on an emotional level, or the first indications of becoming aware of your psychic abilities or trusting your intuition. In recording examples like this, you start to become more aware of your own power and the ways magick works.

If you wish to perform a more structured ritual, that is, following the eight points I mentioned earlier, you will need to do a bit of research as to the various forms of rituals available, and in particular to the wording and directions used. Remember that in the Southern Hemisphere, the sun moves in the opposite direction around the earth to the Northern Hemisphere and, therefore, circle casting is usually performed in a deosil (anti-clockwise) direction. Depending on whether you want to use the elemental guardians, you will also need to find out the most appropriate elemental directions for your area.

The next step is to write a ritual suitable to your needs (although there are numerous rituals available, I do encourage people to write their own rituals, as after all, only you really know your true goal for such a ritual). The ritual provided in the

Appendix can be used as a template when you wish to do this.

Finally, the most important step is to put everything into practice and have a go. A number of people delay performing their own rituals purely out of fear of doing something wrong. Popular Wiccan authors such as Ray Buckland and Scott Cunningham recall, in their books, occasions when they have forgotten the words, or tripped over things. I have also known a number of magical practitioners who use "cheat sheets" when performing a new ritual, myself included. We all learn through trial and error, and it is only through practice, dedication and persistence that we can make our own magick happen.

There are a few instances where it is considered unwise to perform a ritual. These are:

- If you have a weak or damaged aura (due to trauma, substance abuse, etc). I would recommend that maybe you consider seeking counselling or undergo healing under the guidance of a qualified professional.
- If you feel mentally confused. Engage in a basic relaxation or meditation practice instead.
- When you are under the influence of alcohol or recreational drugs. Wait until you are not.
- If your purpose is revenge, anger or hate. Within contemporary witchcraft, it is recommended that your emotions should be calm and that you are clear with your intent for the ritual.
- To show off to your friends. Magick is real – it is not a parlour trick.

Today there are numerous books and internet sites available that contain rituals, and not all are from a contemporary witchcraft or even a Wiccan perspective. If you are intending to use someone else's ritual then make sure that you know what the terms used actually mean. Robert Cochrane, for example, did not call watchtowers in his rituals, he used "castles". Other people may not work with the four elemental forces as known within contemporary witchcraft or Wicca, and may use other forces instead.

It may also be wise not to evoke or invoke deities or forces simply because they sound "cool" or you are wishing to appear "hard core" to your friends (or worse, social media followers), especially if you do not know who they truly are. Remember that these beings, whether they are Gods, spirits, angelic beings or "demons", are higher forces, entities from different realms that may not necessarily "fit" into our preconceived ideals. Research is the key, and know how to at least banish and spiritually protect yourself just in case things do not go according to plan.

Exercise: Undertaking Your First Ritual

- You may like to follow the ritual provided at the Appendix of this book, incorporating the techniques that you have learnt up to now. Before you commence, however, ensure that you have read the ritual format at least a few times to make sure that you are familiar with the process and what you need to do.
- At point 6 of the "Main Body of the Ritual", you might like to simply meditate on how you are feeling, especially if this is your first attempt at casting a circle. Alternatively, you might like to light a special candle and dedicate yourself to the path of contemporary witchcraft. There is an example of a dedication ritual in the Appendix section.

Cone of Power

One thing that I have noticed is that many beginners' books do not mention how to raise a "Cone of Power". Do people still utilise this these days or is it all left up to "intent"? What a cone of power refers to is the energy that is built up in the circle when engaging in ritual. Once the energy is built to a peak, it is then directed into the spell that is to be crafted. This is why a magick circle is cast in the first place - to contain this power or energy.

As we move deosil (anti-clockwise in the Southern Hemisphere and clockwise in the Northern Hemisphere) around our circle, we create energy. The more we focus on this energy, the more it swirls, forming something that is similar to a cone. While the emphasis on the creation of the cone of power tends to be on the specific raising of energy through the reciting of chants such as the "Witches Rune" by Doreen Valiente, and dancing around a focal point, i.e., a cauldron, the energy actually starts to form from the outset of the rite, when you first cast your circle, or even beforehand if you physically sweep your ritual space. It is for this reason that I teach my students how to move in the appropriate direction in circle.

For a solitary I believe the same applies in that you commence creating your cone of power from the very moment that you start to cast your circle. There are also a number of ways that a solitary can build up the energy within their cone:

- **Spinning**. Begin in the east and start by moving slowly in free form spinning. As you move in a deosil direction, turn to your right a few times and then to your left, before repeating both directions. This way you are building energy by balancing it.
- **Tensing your muscles**: Hold your arms out in front of you, with your elbows bent. Squeeze your biceps while you make balls with your fists. As you flex your muscles you should feel the energy in our arms. As you release the muscles, the energy moves from your biceps into your hands and the out into the space in front of you.
- **Dancing**, if your space is large enough, is a great way to raise energy. It also helps to express your inner self.
- **Drumming** or listening to a drumming cd.
- **Chanting**: Stand in front of your altar and chant "aaahhh".

Starting off as deeply as you can with your arms by your side, then as you slowly raise the pitch of your voice, also slowly raise your arms until the pitch of your voice is as high as you can go and your arms are above your head. While raising energy in this fashion, you can also visualise the energy raising around you.

Raise energy in the way that feels appropriate and comfortable to you. Continue to do so, visualising the energy you are raising is swirling and forming a cone both around you and within you, rising to a peak. When the energy has reached the peak, release the cone by directing the energy towards to purpose in which you are working.

If you are new at raising energy, I personally recommend trying the dancing or spinning methods. Dance or spin around your working space until you feel dizzy, then dance or spin some more, but this time bring your focus back to the reason why you have created the ritual. Then again, when you feel dizzy, stop and stand in front of your altar, directing the energy you have raised into your working. It should go without saying that should you have any underlying health issues, then to raise energy through spinning is probably not an appropriate method.

Exercise: Creating an Astral Temple

While astral temples are actually created in your mind as opposed to the astral plane, they are a perfect place to create if you do not have the luxury of having your own ritual space as they offer a place where you can perform rituals, craft spells, commune with spirits or the Gods, or even use as a quiet place to get away from things. Astral temples, like anything created in the mind or astral plane, do require regular maintenance. Therefore, once created, it is recommended that you visit your astral temple at least once a month.

- Spend some time drawing or creating a list of basic attributes that you would like your temple to have. Is it a castle with stone walls, or a crystal temple? A cottage in the woods, or hidden deep within a cave? Consider what materials it is made out of, how it is decorated, views out any of the windows, etc. You might like to print out images from the internet and make a collage.

- Consider how you lock and protect your temple. Will you use an ornate iron key, or do you part the mists like in Marion Zimmer Bradley's novel *Mists of Avalon*? Is there a special password you will need to recite, or touchpad combination?

- Once you decided on the above, ground and centre by following the Four-Fold Breath technique. Cast your circle by following the ritual provided in the Appendix section of this book. When you get to point 6, the main body of the ritual, sit down and visualise yourself in the location where your temple will be built. Begin to build your temple "brick by brick", making sure that first you set a foundation upon which your astral temple will be built.

- Once completed, unlock your temple and walk through it, making any changes or adjustments as you go. You may like to create your altar, decorate the walls or even add carpet to the floor.

- When you have finished, lock your temple, end the meditation, and then continue finishing with the ritual format by opening your circle.

Once built, you can visit your astral temple at any time simply by thinking about it. It will change as you change and as you want it to change. Remember that meditation is key for concentration. It is recommended that your keep your temple clean and free of clutter as much as possible. At the end of the day, creativity is important, because your temple is you.

Four Powers of the Sphinx

It is within *Transcendental Magic: Its Doctrine and Ritual*[46] by French occultist Eliphas Lévi (1810 - 1875) that the magical formula known as the Four Powers of the Sphinx was first mentioned. Although later to become known as the "Magician's Pyramid" or even the "Witch's Pyramid," amongst other names, Lévi referred to these four "powers" as being "indispensable conditions" that a serious practitioner of magick should include within their study in order to attain the "sanctum regnum", or the knowledge and power. These four "powers" form a magical philosophy that underpin everything you need to know n the order to work magick. They were also inscribed upon the symbolic forms of the mystical sphinx as being:

- To know (*sciere*)
- To will (*velle*)
- To dare (*audere*)
- To be silent (*tacere*).

Each of these four powers were linked with each of the four elements (air, fire, earth, and water) as well as the four kerubic, or fixed, signs of the zodiac (Aquarius, Taurus, Leo and Scorpio). The sphinx itself is a composite creature, as it has the head of a man, the torso and front paws of a lion, the rear end of a bull, and the wings of the eagle. According to Lévi, this mysterious beast symbolized the synthesis and synergy of the "four powers" that were represented by the "four living creatures of symbolism" (the kerubs) who have been "conquered and enchained" into one figure, that being the sphinx.

While both human (i.e., the witch) and the sphinx are composed of the four elements, within the sphinx these elements are balanced, whereas they are not within the human being.

Therefore, the sphinx represents the "perfected man or woman", the magical practitioner in the state of perfection.

Within his final work *The Great Secret: Or Occultism Unveiled*[47], Lévi instructed how to practically apply the Four Powers of the Sphinx, as he states:

> "The great secret of magic, the unique and incommunicable Arcana, has for its purpose the placing of supernatural power at the service of the human will in some way.
> To attain such an achievement it is necessary to KNOW what has to be done, to WILL what is required, to DARE what must be attempted and to KEEP SILENT with discernment."

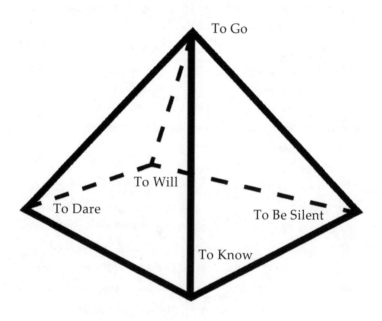

Within contemporary witchcraft, the Four Powers of the Sphinx are often considered to be the cornerstones to magick and are applied as follows:

- **To Know** (*sciere*, relates to the element of air): Know what you are going to do, what is needed, what your intent is, and what repercussions could be. It is important to accumulate as much knowledge of the diverse nature concerning the occult path as you can, as there is power in knowledge for its own sake.

All manner of related subjects can only assist you in your work – things of an anthropological, religious, philosophic nature; works by other occultists; material pertinent to affirm what you learn, i.e., astrology, numerology, Tarot, herbalism and the healing arts in general, mythology, history, and so on.

- **To Will** (*velle*, relates to the element of fire): A disciplined Will is needed to charge a magical tool, cast a circle or direct energy. In its lesser form, the Will of a properly trained witch is capable of directing their lives to their satisfaction. In its greater form, the Will should be capable, in rare circumstances, of directing the course of events beyond themselves, e.g., the environmental destruction (man-made) or in cases of threat, either personal or planetary. In all cases, the energy raised is for defence rather than attack.

  Regular meditation practice teaches how to focus the mind, which fuels your magick much more effectively. Have confidence in your magical working for it to work. Believe that you have done "real" magick and that it works. Your magical working feeds off thoughts and energy, and if you do not feed it, it will die.

- **To Dare** (*audere*, relates to the element of water): Put your knowledge into practice. Infuse your magical working with the energy of emotion. If you do not care about the outcome, then why should the Gods? The same goes for any other ritual or magical working performing. Understand the rituals fully instead of repeating them in parrot fashion.

- **To Be Silent** (*tacere*, relates to the element of earth): When working magick, if you dwell on whether your magick is working or not, you are in effect taking energy away from your working. Let your magick do its work. Also, be discerning as to whom you share details of your workings with, for there are those who seek power for the sake of power itself, and may even instill self-doubt into you, thus taking away your power for their own gratification. Therefore, speak not of what you know until you become that which you seek to serve.

Jessica Bell, better known by the pseudonym of Lady Sheba, described these four powers as being the foundation of witch power in that:

"The first of the four so-called sides of the pyramid is your dynamic, controlled will; the second, your imagination or the ability to see your desire accomplished; third, unshakable and absolute faith in your ability to accomplish anything you desire; and fourth, secrecy."[48]

Bell further reminds the reader the "power shared is power lost", and was of the opinion that the four powers contained with the sphinx were the "basic requirements for the working of witchcraft".

With Lévi's and Lady Sheba's instructions in mind, at times I find myself questioning the need some modern witches have in eagerly exposing intimate details about their practices, especially on social media, where it is not uncommon to see photographs of altars, details of spells and rituals, or even the end product of magical workings. Could it be that in the century that has passed since Lévi these powers are deemed no longer valid in our inter-global mass-media focused society? Or something much worse – that the art of dedicating oneself to a spiritual or magical path is fast becoming a thing of the past, an "outdated" or even "unnecessary" requirement for, as I have been informed on various occasions, nothing is secret these days, for all the mysteries are known. I personally disagree with this assumption. Whilst my life is just as busy and hectic as the next person's, continuing my study of the magical arts and endless perfection of my Craft in order to attain the "sanctum regnum" will always remain high on my list of priorities, just as knowing when to abide by the Four Powers of the Sphinx.

Working with the Moon

The moon has always been considered as a mysterious and powerful force. It moves the tides and guides the flow of the universal energies. As humans, we are made up of a high percentage of water or fluid, and so the moon also affects us, especially women who, away from artificial light, will find that their own bleeding will often coincide with certain phases of the moon. In learning about the moon and its influences, magick can be used to join with the magick of the moon.

From our view point on earth, the moon comes and goes through a process of waxing and waning known as the lunar phases. The new moon, which starts the cycle, is virtually invisible. In the days that follow, more of the moon is revealed to us as it makes its journey around the earth. Halfway through the cycle, the moon is completely illuminated, before it starts to wane until it disappears from sight, only to have the cycle start again.

The moon goes around the earth in 27.3 days, or 27 days seven hours 43 minutes, on average. However, because of the earth's motion around the sun, a complete moon cycle appears to take a couple of days longer: 29.5305882 days to be exact. This number is called the synodic period or "lunation", and is relative to the Sun.

As the moon goes through the eight phases, each last about three and a half days. Starting from the first sliver that appears in our skies, the moon slowly increases in size. As it increases, so its energy also grows. It is, therefore, during these waxing phases of the moon, we can focus on bringing things into our lives, and for starting new projects. The first phase is that of the new moon, which lasts for up to three and a half days. Both the solar and lunar energies are combined in this phase. The new moon offers the opportunity to start planning those long- and short-term goals.

As the sliver of the moon grows, it becomes a crescent that faces to the east in the Southern Hemisphere (west facing if you reside in the Northern Hemisphere). This period is referred to as the crescent moon, from three and a half days to seven days after the new moon, and is the time for gathering information, ideas and the laying of foundations for any upcoming projects. It is also a good time to focus on business, change, emotions and feminine strength.

During the next three and a half day days, the moon is in its first quarter. The time has arrived to speed up those things which may be lagging, and push towards their manifestation. The focus of this phase is on continued success, or to bring the success on faster, to work on friendships, relationships and general good luck.

The final phase before the full moon is the gibbous moon, which is from ten-and-a-half to 14 days after the new moon. This is the time to do some contemplation on what we really "need" to bring into our lives as opposed to things we merely "want".

The full moon happens 14 days after the new moon and is the time when the lunar energies are at their peak, as the moon is directly opposite the sun. The energy of the full moon can be used for many things such as families, knowledge, love or romance, protection, health and healing, motivation, and self-improvement. As this time the moon's energies are at their peak; to capture their power, timing is extremely important. The moon can actually look full in the sky for up to three days, so the most reliable way of finding out when the moon is at its peak is use an astrological calendar or almanac which will give the exact time. This is because after the time given, the moon's energies start to slowly diminish. Therefore, when working magick, it is recommended that you should time your rite so that it is before the time listed.

From the full moon to the dark moon, the moon deceases in

size. As it decreases, so does its energy. Therefore, these are the waning phases of the moon and the time to focus on reducing or removing things from our lives. The first phase after the full moon is known as the disseminating moon. As the moon's energy is beginning to wane, the time has arrived to begin removing obstacles, negative thoughts and emotions, even stress from our lives.

From seven to ten-and-a-half days after the full moon, is the last quarter, and in our skies in the Southern Hemisphere the crescent faces the west. Use this time to disentangle yourself from awkward or uncomfortable situations, for overcoming addictions or debilitating physical problems. Some people even use this phase for divorce proceedings or to neutralise enemies.

The last phase of the moon is the dark moon, from ten-and-a-half to 14 days after the full moon when the moon does not appear to be in the sky at all. This is the time where it is often recommended that no magick should be performed, that we should rest. After all, the moon appears to be resting in our skies. If you want to take advantage of this time, however, it provides a great opportunity to go within ourselves and to find out who we really are, and to analyse on deeper levels the things we want. It is also a good time to focus on psychic abilities, to learn divination skills, or even analyse what our subconscious is trying to tell us through our dreams.

The following information has been adapted from my forthcoming book, *On Her Silver Rays: Moon, Magic and Myth of the Queen of Heavens and the Starry Skies*[49], and details each of the moon phases with how they are used within contemporary witchcraft:

- **New** (from the day of the new moon to 3.5 days after, 0-45° ahead of sun): From when the first sliver appears in the sky, this is the new moon. The moon rises at dawn, sets at sunset.

The sun and moon energies are combined in this phase to give great strength to new projects. Spells and magical workings performed around this time should focus on self-improvement, employment, health, farms and gardens, and romance

- **Crescent** (from 3.5 to 7 days after new moon, 45-90º ahead of sun). The moon is 1-49% visible to the left. The moon rises at mid-morning, sets after sunset, therefore it can only be seen for a short time after the sun goes down.

  Perform drawing, increasing or growth spells and magical workings that include enhancing goals and projects, anything related to animals, business, change, emotions, and matriarchal strength. The new moon is a good time for new ventures, initiating new projects, as well as love and health.

- **First Quarter/Waxing** (from 7 to 10.5 days after new moon, 90-135° ahead of sun). The moon is 50% visible to the left. The moon rises at noon, sets at midnight.

  Time to put on a little extra power to things and push forward towards manifestation, focus on success, health and partnerships. Magical workings include courage, elemental magic, friendships, and motivation.

- **Gibbous** (from 10.5 to 14 days after new moon, 135-180° ahead of sun). The moon is 51-99% visible to the left. The moon rises at mid-afternoon, sets around 3.00am.

  Time to catch loose ends or make necessary changes. Magical workings include drawing, increasing, or growth.

- **Full** (14 days after new moon, 180-135° behind the sun). The moon is 100% visible. The moon rises sunset, sets at dawn.

  Time for prophecy, protection, healing and celebration. Magical workings include love and romance, artistic endeavours, families, gaining knowledge, self-empowerment, self-improvement, legal undertakings and psychic matters.

- **Disseminating** (3 to 7 days after the full moon, 135-90° behind the sun). The moon is 50% visible to the right. The moon rises mid-evening, sets at mid-morning.

    Time to commence waning, repelling, decreasing, or reversing spells, remove negativity, Magical workings include overcoming addictions, ending bad habits, and ending emotional situations such as divorce proceedings, stress and anxiety.

- **Last Quarter/Waning** (7 to 10 days after the full moon, 90-45° behind the sun). The moon is -49% visible to the right. The moon rises at midnight, sets at noon.

    Time to release any negativity, continue banishing work or to support previous banishing ritual. Magical workings include addictions, protection, finalising divorce proceedings, and banishing ill health and stress.

- **Dark** (from 11 to 14 days after the full moon, 45-0° behind the sun). The moon rises at 3.00 am, sets at mid-afternoon, so it is not visible in the night's sky.

    Time to move within yourself, to understand anger and passion and steering them to work in a positive way. Magical workings include addictions, enemies, quarrels, justice, divorce, removing obstacles, physical problems, stopping stalkers and theft.

Within contemporary witchcraft, the 13 gatherings that are traditionally held which are aligned with the full moon are referred to as "esbats". The word is derived from the Old French word *s'esbattre* (Modern French ébat) meaning "frolic, to amuse oneself or diversion." It was Dr Margaret Murray who first associated an esbat with a gathering of witches that occurred at a time other than a sabbat (the seasonal observances). I tend to hold my esbats just prior to the actual date of the full moon to ensure that I have encapsulated the full energy of the moon. When I calculate the dates and times of moon phases, one internet site I use is Time and Date (https://www.timeanddate.com).

Understanding Moon Folk Names

The full moon is often associated with folk names, and due to social media, the focus of these names tends to be those originating from America. Early European settlers noticed that the Native Americans kept track of time by using both solar and lunar calendars where each lunar month was given a name for the full moon appearing during the cycle, often reflecting seasonal conditions or activities. The settlers subsequently adopted many of those names into their own folklore, as well as adding some of their own. Over time, the full moons that made up the yearly lunar cycle were known by an assortment of different names. Some are given below:

- **January**: Wolf Moon (named after the howling of hungry wolves). Other names include Winter Moon, Old Moon, Cold Weather Moon, Ice Moon, and Trees Broken Moon.
- **February**: Snow Moon (due to the amount of snow on the ground). Other names include Hunger Moon, Storm Moon, and Wind Moon.
- **March**: Worm Moon (named after the worm trails that would appear in the newly thawed ground). Other names include Storm Moon, Crow Moon, Chaste Moon, and Wind Strong Moon.
- **April**: Pink Moon (due to the early blossoming wild flower). Other names include Wind Moon, Planter's Moon, Deep Water Moon, and Sprouting Grass Moon.
- **May**: Flower Moon (due to the number of abundant flowers). Other names include Hare Moon, Corn Planting Moon, and Moon of the Shedding Ponies.
- **June**: Strawberry Moon (time for harvesting strawberries). Other names include Strong Sun Moon, Honey Moon, Hot

Moon, and Corn Moon.

- **July**: Buck Moon (when stags lose their antlers to regrow new ones). Other names include Blessing Moon, Thunder Moon, Hay Moon, Mead Moon, Rain Moon, and Red Salmon Time Moon.
- **August**: Sturgeon Moon (when this species of fish is abundant). Other names include Corn Moon, Dog's Day Moon, Wart Moon, Red Moon, and Wheat Cut Moon.
- **September**: Harvest Moon (when crops are gathered). Other names include Dying Grass Moon, Barley Moon, and Little Wind Moon.
- **October**: Hunter's Moon (marked the time for hunting of animals). Other names include Blood Moon, Deer Rutting Season Moon, Basket Moon, and Falling River Moon.
- **November**: Beaver Moon (when traps were set for beavers or when the beavers were active in building their dams). Other names include Mourning Moon, Frost Moon, and Killing Deer Moon.
- **December**: Cold Moon (marking the coming of winter). Other names include Long Nights Moon, Ashes Fire Moon, and Big Freezing Moon.

The joy of social media is that there tends to be an increasing lack of personal research and this can often be seen when referring to the folk names that the moon is known by. An example of this is for people to talk about the "Wolf Moon" in January in Australia, a country that does not and never has had wolves. Likewise, I have noticed the September full moon being referred to as the "Worm Moon". Whilst logic seems to indicate that this has occurred by moving the Northern Hemispheric folk name around by six months, the problem is that September does not generate a similar thaw in Australia for worm trails to be noticed. I am sure that for some readers living in the Northern Hemisphere, the same could very well apply.

Exercise: Moon Names

Instead of attempting to adapt Northern Hemispheric folk names for the moon, I encourage my students to make regular observances of what is happening in their own local environment in order to come up with their own list of names. For example, as March marks the time of the grape harvest in the Barossa wine region, Harvest Moon or Grape Moon may seem appropriate; August usually marks the time that the almond trees begin to flower so Almond Bud Moon could be used; and while not native to Australia, November is often marked by the beautiful pale lilac flower of the jacaranda (*Jacaranda mimosifolia*) trees, so I refer to November's full moon as "Jacaranda Moon".

If you live in the Northern Hemisphere, do the folk names reflect the moon with your environment? For example, what would reflect the August Moon to your environment especially if you are an urban dweller?

It is interesting to note that within many Australian Aboriginal communities, the moon is perceived as male and some traditional stories tell of the sun woman pursuing the moon man across the sky from day to day, occasionally meeting during an eclipse.[50] This might be something to consider if you wish to align yourself with a particular pantheon as not all perceive the moon as female.

Using Herbs, Incenses and Colour

Considering that the plant kingdom developed on earth millions of years before the evolution of human beings, it is fair to say that herbs are the oldest magical tools in existence, with their beneficial properties with respect to both physical and spiritual well-being having been incorporated into the practices of healers, shamans, and other medicine men and women for millennia.

A witch uses herbs in many ways – in the concoction of herbal potions and elixirs, in gris-gris (herbal charm) bags and dream pillows, smudging, through the use of oils and herbal extracts, and probably more commonly as incense. As the amount of information about using herbs can be overwhelming, I recommend the works of Paul Beyerl and Scott Cunningham (listed in the bibliography). The latter's books often form the basis of magical herbal information found on many websites. British witch Anna Franklin also has a wonderful *Heath Witch's Compendium* that is highly recommended for readers wishing to fully incorporate the use of botanicals into their life.

Eight more commonly used herbs within contemporary witchcraft are:

- **Mugwort** (*Artemisia vulgaris*): Aids in strengthening psychic powers, prophetic dreaming, and astral projection and can also be used for protection and healing.
- **White Sage** (*Salvia apiana*): Cleansing and purifying your sacred space, magical tools, Tarot cards, crystals; banishing negativity and enhance learning, knowledge. Normal garden sage (*Salvia officinalis*) should not be used as a substitute for white sage.
- **Bay** (*Laurus nobilis*): Enhances clairvoyance, induces prophetic dreaming, used for protection and purification.
- **Rosemary** (*Rosmarinus officinalis*): Protection, purification,

healing, and love.

- **Lavender** (*Lavandula*): For good luck, attracting love, prophetic dreaming.
- **Clove** (*Syzygium aromaticum*): To cleanse objects, increase positive energy, protection and mental clarity.
- **Cinnamon** (*Cinnamomum verum*): Enhances spirituality, success, luck, protection and prosperity.
- **Eucalyptus:** Used in smoking ceremonies by Aboriginal peoples, it has purification and protection properties, brings in fresh energy, heals regrets and worries, relieves mental exhaustion. Despite its abundance, eucalyptus tends to be overlooked with the preference being white sage or frankincense and more recently palo santo.

While not an herb, salt is an important ingredient that is used within contemporary witchcraft, in particularly for consecrating ritual spaces (as a representative of earth) as well as for its protective abilities. During the Middle Ages salt was used to ward off evil spirits and people even put salt in their chimneys to prevent demons from entering their houses. However, the use of salt predates this. The ancient Egyptians considered salt to be so sacred that they offered it to their Gods, as well as using it in their embalming practices. The Romans considered salt to be a symbol of wisdom and used it in their baptism rituals.

My personal preference is to use sea or coarse salt as opposed to table salt (which is iodised). There are other salts that are used within magic including "black salt" (usually composed of cauldron scrapings, charcoal and salt that creates a protective barrier and is used in banishment and hex breaking rituals), the pink Himalayan salt (used for cleansing and healing), and various other dyed salts that incorporate the magical correspondences of colour.

Exercise: Making a Gris-Gris Bag

Pronounced "gree-gree", this term refers to both the making of the charm and the charm itself, that originated in Africa, particularly Ghana and Senegal. These bags were made out of red flannel, chamois or leather, filled with specific herbs, stone, bones, coins and even carved stones to ward off bad luck and evil spirits. In New Orleans, gris gris are often hidden from public view, are always prepared within a ritual before an altar, and are then consecrated to the four elements – earth, air, fire and water. It is also said that the number of items placed into a gris gris should be an odd number, never less than three yet never more than 13.

Colour symbolism is important and should be chosen to depict your need (see list on the following pages). All the items chosen to be placed in the bag should be specific to the desired purpose and the bag should be anointed with an appropriate oil. A specifically chosen charm should be recited while making the gris gris as the words will create the energy that will become a part of the bag itself. The final act is to breathe upon the gris gris to give it life.

An example of a gris gris bag for financial abundance is made from green material and contains a piece of citrine (renowned for its money drawing abilities), a pinch of basil and cinquefoil, a piece of galangal root, some shavings of angelica root, three silver coins, and a small magnet. Ginger oil was used to anoint the bag relating to its ability to increase finances, prosperity, and power. I wrote a following chant to be recited when the gris gris was being made:

"On the waning moon my problems cease
As prosperity comes to me
Basil and citrine draws to me
Financial abundance to set me free."

Using Incense

The word "incense" is derived from the Latin *incendere*, meaning "to burn". Raw resins, such as frankincense and myrrh, have long been burnt to cleanse and purify sacred spaces, including churches. There are many forms of incenses available today – joss sticks, cones, resins, or even specifically blended concoctions – all of which can be used to aid your magical workings. If you desire to use granulated or powered incense, you will need a charcoal disk in order to burn the incense upon. These disks can be purchased from Middle Eastern supermarkets as they are used in hookah or shisha pipes. They may also be found in some new age, health or even smoke product stores. You will also need some kind of fire proof container, commonly known as a censer, in which to burn the incense. An old clay bowl purchased from a second hand or charity store alternatively can be used.

During your magical working, you can burn granulated resins, a variety of dried herbs of the appropriate correspondence, or a ready-mixed incense that you can purchase from various stores and online. Some of the more common are:

- **Frankincense** (*Boswellia sacra*): Spicy but sweet aroma. Associated with purification, protection, joy, celebration, meditation, consecration, solar energy.
- **Myrrh** (*Commiphora myrrha*): Bitter sweet aroma. Associated with sanctity, honouring the spirits, purification, healing, as well as heightening the vibration and power of any magical working.
- **Benzoin** (*Styrax benzoin*): Light clean scent. Associated with purification, healing, prosperity and general attraction.
- **Copal** (*Burseraceae*): Light, sweet aroma. Associated with love, house blessings, dedication and meditation, celebration, solar energy and creating a sacred space.
- **Dragon's Blood** (*Dracaena draco*): Sweet, soft and slightly amber-like aroma. Associated with protection, purification

and can boost energy in all magical workings.

If you decide to use charcoal and granulated or powered incense, the following should be noted:

- Use a pair of tweezers or a small pair of tongs to hold the charcoal disk while lighting it in order to prevent burning your fingers.
- It is a good idea to light the charcoal disk either outside or under an exhaust fan due to the amount of smoke initially produced as the saltpetre ignites. Charcoal disks usually contain self-igniting ingredient such as saltpetre (Potassium nitrate) that cause the brick to smoke and even spark. It is recommended that you light charcoal disks in a well-ventilated space, and be aware of the smoke, especially if you are asthmatic or have other sensitivities, or if there are smoke detectors in your ritual space.
- Place your censer on a tile should you wish to carry it around the circle during your magical working, especially if you use a brass censer, as these can heat up very quickly. The tile will also protect any wooden surface your censer may be placed upon.
- Before putting any resins or powered incense on the charcoal disk, allow the brick to burn across the top, leaving behind a thin layer of grey ash. This ensures even burning.
- You only need to use a small amount of resin incense at a time.
- When it comes to storing your charcoal disks, I recommend you use an airtight container, such as an old coffee jar or zip lock bag to prevent them from getting damp. I have also found that if stored this way, the charcoal disks tend to last longer.

There are an abundance of scents when it comes to joss sticks and incense cones so what you use will depend on your own personal preference. If I am using incense as simply a means to provide a pleasant scent to the room for meditation or relaxation, then my personal preference is to use Indian temple joss sticks that are made from natural ingredients as opposed to the more fashionable (and often artificial) scents. Satya is probably one of my favourite brands, especially their Sai Baba Nag Champa and Dragon's Fire (a bit soft in aroma than Dragon's Blood). If I wish to burn a joss stick with respect to the ritual or magical working that I am undertaking, then my preference is to use the Auroshikha brand.

Using Colour

The use of colour in ritual can be an important aspect to consider, as metaphysically colours hold different energies and therefore can be used for specific purposes. Colour can be incorporated in your altar cloth, the colour of material used or gris-gris bags, candles, crystals and the like. While there are many different colour associations, the following list is what I personally use:

- **White**: Cleansing, understanding, spiritual growth, a basic stand-in colour.
- **Black**: Transformation; banishing and releasing negative energies.
- **Red**: Love (passion), energy, fighting spirit (competition), sometimes health, relates to the element of fire.
- **Orange**: Mental, study, encouragement and power.
- **Yellow**: Communication, ideas and decisions, energising (sun), relates to the element of air.
- **Green**: Money, abundance, prosperity, fertility, gaining employment.
- **Blue**: Healing, psychic intensifying, relates to the element of water.

- **Purple**: Divination, psychic abilities, spiritual healing, dreams, lunar (moon) workings.
- **Silver**: Psychic development, meditation, warding off negativity, lunar (moon) workings.
- **Gold**: Health, success, divination, good fortune, solar (sun) workings
- **Brown**: Balance, grounding, home, animals, employment.
- **Grey**: Binding negative influences, complex decision-making.
- **Pink**: Love (of the self, romantic), spiritual awakening, friendships.

The Art of Psychic Defence

Humankind has always felt the presence of negativity. Frightening dreams, mental illness, fatigue and just plain old bad luck are all caused by the presence of negativity in our lives. In ancient times, negativity was believed to have been caused by demons and evil spirits. Today we know that the causes of negativity are many, and that perspective plays a large part in its existence. Sometimes "bad luck" is actually a karmic process of cleansing, but because such a process is generally misunderstood, such a cleansing process is seen as negativity. Any form of anger or violence will generate negative energies that can be felt long after the actual act has passed.

Other people can be sources of negativity to us, even though they may mean no harm. They drain us of our vitality, leaving us with little energy. These people are known as "psychic vampires", and most of them are unaware of what they are doing. Heavy paranoia and extreme pessimism will also create tangible negative energies, either from others or our own selves.

Regardless of the possible causes of negativity, the acknowledgment of its existence is what is important to the magical practitioner. Simply examining the sources of negativity will not make it go away – denying it access to your personal power will. Psychic protection will help you to do this, on the spiritual, mental and physical levels.

Methods of Protection

There are numerous forms of protection that are used within contemporary witchcraft. The following are just some examples that you may come across:

- **Protection Charms**: The "Law of Symbolism" advises that many symbols have a power beyond our conscious knowledge and have been used throughout the ages for protection. To Christians, the cross is a symbol of God's protection. Before it, the equal-armed cross, a symbol of sacredness and balance, was a protective symbol.

Certain minerals and crystals are known for their protective properties. Sea salt is used in many charms. Iron grounds harmful energy like a lightning rod. Dark coloured crystals, such as obsidian, smoky quartz and onyx are protective. Fluorite helps amplify your energy field to create a protective boundary or border. It also cleanses your energy field of harmful energy, like an energy purifier. Black tourmaline is another crystal well-known for its protective properties. Other protective charms include the making of witch's bottles, herbal gris-gris bags, hanging horse shoes, etc.

- **Incense**: Using frankincense and myrrh as frankincense resonates with the energy of the God, and myrrh with the energy of the Goddess. Together they create a unified vibration. The Catholic Church uses it for similar reasons. Native Americans use combinations of sage, sweetgrass and cedar. Copal, a resin from Mexico that is similar to frankincense, is the favoured incense of Central and South America. Lavender, cinnamon, cloves, palo santo and pine resins also create sacred space. Here in Australia, eucalyptus leaves have long been used by the Aboriginal people in their cleansing ceremonies.
- **Banishing Earth Pentagram**. (See the Appendix for list of pentagrams).
- **The Tower of Light** exercise (later in this section).
- **Calling upon Spiritual Guardians**.
- **Ritual cleansing** of area and ritual bathing of self.
- **Rock salt in a glass of water** that is then placed in the corner of a room and emptied on a regular basis (i.e., once a week).

- **Laughter**.

Exercise: The Tower of Light

This exercise is a form of passive psychic self-defence, which involves active meditation using visualisation. It should be done at least every day, better still twice (upon waking and before retiring). With practice, the visualisation is easily performed and can be called upon in an emergency when needed. Each step of this exercise serves an important function and should not be omitted. Some people refer to the following exercise as "shielding."

- Stand erect, feet shoulder-width, arms at your sides, breathing evenly and deeply. Relax your body, from the top of your head working slowly down to your feet.
- Visualise that you are surrounded by a sphere of intense blue light that extends about 20cm outwardly from every point on the surface of your body.
- Continue to maintain this image and visualise a globe of brilliant white light above (but not touching) your head. The globe is inside of your bright blue aura.
- Concentrate on this bright white globe so that it becomes brighter, glowing white like burning magnesium.
- Next, feel the white globe showering you with glittering white light filled with silver sparkles. This white light should permeate your entire being, coursing vibrantly through you.
- The outer shell of your aura should be an intense bright blue filled with the vibrant, sparkling white light. Concentrate on this complete image as long as you can, fully believing in its reality. Feel your outer auric shell as a hard, sharply defined blue as you feel blissful and alert.
- As you close, let the image fade slowly, but not from reality.

There are many variants to the above exercise, but they ultimately aim to have the same result - that is, to strengthen our aura. This is important, because it is our aura that alerts us to an unfavourable environment where we may need to protect ourselves.

The image of white light is recognised in nearly all belief systems: in Christianity it is the light of the halo - of divinity. In *The Tibetan Book of Living and Dying*[51], the reader is instructed to tell the soul of the deceased to walk into the white light, as opposed to the darker, coloured lights that will surround it. To the Tibetan Buddhists, the act of putting aside human fear and entering the white light is part of a process that will enable the soul to escape the wheel of rebirth. The white light is viewed as the light, symbol or energy of Godhead, and its use as a method of protection has grown in popularity with the "New Age" movement.

Insights into Spellcrafting

Some people associate witchcraft purely with spellcrafting, but in truth, spellcrafting is only a small aspect. When looking back on the path I have been following for the last thirty or so years, I can almost count the number of actual spells performed on one hand. The reason for this is that I tend to perceive life as the great teacher and while I may use magick to help me understand why certain obstacles or occurrences happen in my life, I do not tend to use magick to avoid such experiences - taking the good and the bad. Also, a lot of what I have seen in books or on the internet called "spells" I would personally classify as rituals. At the end of the day, it is all about learning and growing through experiences. When it comes to actual spellcrafting, you have to be completely certain of what you desire. I am sure that many readers have heard the saying: "Be careful what you wish for as it may come true." This saying rings true in magick.

Today there is a large array of spiritual, esoteric and magical knowledge available to us, and all we need to do is simply adapt this knowledge in a way we feel comfortable with, and which is fitting to our own particular belief system. So how can you encompass the ancient techniques of spellcrafting if your religion frowns upon the use of magick? The answer to this is that we all, regardless of whatever religious or spiritual path we follow, actually perform similar acts; we only refer to them by different names.

Consider for a moment – what is the most important aspect to make a prayer or a spell work? The simple answer for both is belief. For a prayer, it is the belief in a higher force (i.e., God) who will hear your request and then bring it into your life. For a spell, it is the belief that certain ingredients have magical properties that will subsequently bring your request into your life. You must also have belief in magick. This is strengthened by faith that your magick will work. If you do not believe 100% in magick and your ability, then any doubt will actually detract from your magical working, making it less effective. Doubt works against your magick and your own ability – and therefore defeating the purpose. So, if you doubt your ability and whether or not magick works, then maybe you should think again before attempting to craft any kind of spell.

When you say a prayer or perform a spell, you are identifying something you want to do or you want done. In sympathetic magick, the witch will have something which is linked to the object of the spell, and what they do to that thing is considered to happen to the object of the spell. This action activates your own personal energy and directs it towards your goal. It is ideal to magnify your personal power with the forces which you have called upon during the ritual. A major purpose of a spell, after all, is to build power and energy, and then direct it to its goal.

There are numerous ways in which you can build up your personal energy or power, but the spoken word is probably one of the easiest or most effective techniques. The repetition of chants or mantras not only strengthens the belief in what you are doing (i.e., spellcrafting), but can also help open the doorways to the hidden realms, enabling communication with spirit guides, the higher self, or other teachers who are not of the physical plane. In magick, repetition strengthens the power of the spell.

Although it is ideal to craft a spell under specific ritualised situations, this is not always necessary. A spell can be said a specific number of times, a technique which is common throughout various parts of the world where certain numbers are considered potent. A spell can be also be said and then blown on a particular charm, amulet or talisman. I constantly see deeply religious people whisper a prayer while holding their crucifixes and then kiss their chosen talisman. I am sure that they would not consider that what they are doing is a form of spellcrafting, but, in essence, this is actually what they are doing.

Always use positive statements – never use negatives. For example, do not say "I do not want to be unemployed"; instead say "I want a job". Better still declare "I have the job I am best suited to", or "I am gainfully employed in my chosen profession". Always visualise a positive outcome to your desire. If you want to craft a spell to obtain a new job, visualise yourself in your chosen position being contented. You also need to be realistic. While you might be able to obtain that perfect job through the use of crafting a spell, no amount of magick will keep you in that position if you are not qualified, have the appropriate experience, or if you abuse your position.

Remember that as there are no scapegoats in witchcraft, you and you alone are fully responsible for any outcome of any spell or ritual working that you have undertaken. It is strongly recommended, therefore, that prior to any spellcrafting, you spend time determining the exact outcome you wish to achieve. This is because the Gods and universe work in mysterious ways and not necessarily aligned to your way of thinking. If you simply do a spell for money, for example, then that could range from finding $5.00 in your jacket pocket that you forgot about, to having to work an excessive amount of overtime. You may even find yourself obtaining money through some kind of insurance claim (or worse). Likewise, a spell for obtaining more peace in your life may result in the severing of relationships, as you realise that these no longer serve you in a positive way. More often than not, the universe will provide us with what we need and not exactly what we want.

Another point is that not every occasion can, or should be, rectified by spell or magical working. For mental health issues, for example, you should see your local doctor and get a referral to a counsellor or psychologist or another health care professional. If abusive or threatening behaviour is a problem, then maybe register a complaint with the police. As I have pointed out previously, witchcraft is about taking self-responsibility, so be a responsible witch and seek professional assistance whenever necessary. This is because magick is real and as such it should be treated with respect. Until you fully know what you are doing and understand the energies you are working with, then (at least in my view) it is wise to err on the side of caution, especially if you are a solitary or are not in contact with a more experienced magical practitioner.

When it comes to the actual spell itself, it is not advisable to blindly copy someone else's spell. This includes those found in books, on the internet, or even from so-called experts on magical practices found in magazines. When you copy someone else's spell, you can never be sure of the full intention of that person, the circumstances, and even the desired goal. While it may be tempting to take the easier option and use a spell that someone else has already crafted, there is only one person who truly knows your true desire and motivation, and that person is yourself. By all means adapt your spell from another whereby you personalise it. What you are doing in this respect is adding your own power to it. This is after all the whole purpose behind spellcrafting – the adding of something of yours to it.

The art of spellcrafting does not begin when you actually perform the spell. It begins when you first desire to craft one. From that point onwards, everything you do, from researching appropriate words and items that you may need to use to the actual action, strengthens your magick. The more of your own unique energy that you put into the spell, then the more tailor-made it will be to your own specific desire.

One of the core elements to spellcrafting, especially from a contemporary witchcraft perspective, is the personal study and effort that the individual witch puts into their craft. It may be extremely enticing to the neophyte to want to perform spells straight away. However, it is recommended that you are first familiar with the ways of magick and in particular any possible consequences when it comes to spellcrafting (the latter occurs regardless of whether you believe in code of ethics such as the Wiccan Rede). If you are going to call upon specific Gods, it is advisable to ensure that you have established a connection or relationship with them first, or at least know what they are associated with; likewise, when it comes to elemental and angelic beings, spirits, and other such entities. This is because performing magick without properly understanding and thoroughly researching the subject matter can be dangerous to yourself, as well as those around you if you do not completely know what you are doing.

When you put the time into learning something, it assists you to develop not only a deeper knowledge and understanding of that topic, but even a better appreciation. It encourages spiritual growth and wisdom resulting in you being more likely to retain the information you have learnt in your memory than you otherwise would from copying someone else's work. This leads to you being more successful in your spellcrafting, as you are able to incorporate different things that you have learned, which allows you to tweak spells to be more powerful. This in turn leads to you developing stronger intuition and therefore less likely to need to refer to books, especially as timing is often an important aspect when it comes to spellcrafting.

It is often recommended that you should take into consideration what phase the moon is in, because this can influence the outcome of your spellwork. When the moon is waxing, growing in size from the first sliver after the dark moon to when it is full, this is the time to increase things in your life, or to bring things to you. After the full moon to when the moon disappears from the night's sky, this is the waning phase and should be used to banish or remove things from your life. But once again, consider the desired outcome of your spell. If you desire to lose weight, then the waxing moon can be used to increase fitness and healthy attitudes. By simply using the waning moon to "lose weight", you may find yourself doing just this but through some kind of serious illness. Personal import is needed, i.e., changing your dietary habits and exercising, as you cannot rely on magick alone if you want a longer-lasting or even permanent change.

Once a spell is crafted, give it time to work, and in the meantime, get on with your life. After a given time, such as a full lunar cycle, you can see what results have been obtained. As mentioned earlier, the universe does work in subtle ways, so finding money down the back of the couch as opposed to winning a lottery will mean your money spell has worked.

When you record your spell in your magical diary or journal, include your initial intent, the phase of the moon, whether you used any specific herbs, crystals, oils and the like. This will form a reference that you can return to and build upon at a later stage. You can also add other information in this book as well, turning it into your own personal Book of Shadows. Knowledge of the magical and esoteric meanings of herbs, crystals and the like can be obtained from a variety of books and other sources such as the internet. However, do not take everything you read on face value. Experiment for yourself and try and see what specific herbs and crystals, for example, relate to various lunar phases, magical workings, planets and so on. You may find that your own correspondences do not always match those given in other resources. It is okay because it is your spell after all, and how you craft it is up to you entirely, and not someone else.

Keep your magical workings secret and to yourself. By this I mean that you should not, after crafting a spell, tell your family and friends about it. Such action distracts the power from the spell and depending in the opinions of others, may also harbour doubts, especially if the people you tell do not believe in magick. The same applies to sharing your magical workings on social media until the desired goal has been achieved. Remember the Four Powers of the Sphinx.

Once you have crafted your spell, you may think that you can sit back and let the universe bring things to you. However, it does not work a simply as that. You still need to personally add things to your spellcrafting. For example, if you want to obtain a job, you will still need to read the newspapers, write the applications and go to the interviews in the appropriate clothing. While it may be your desire to secure a particular job, remember that it is also the desire of the interviewers to secure the most appropriate person for that particular position. Be realistic in your approach. If you do not have the skills, qualifications or experience, you are not going to land such a position. Also craft a spell for a position which you are most suited for or a position which will lead you, once you have obtained the necessary qualifications and experience, to your dream position. There is only one way to climb a mountain and that begins with the first step.

When you have obtained your desired outcome through your spellcrafting, I consider it to be very important to give thanks. If I have crafted a spell that has resulted in a monetary outcome, I always make sure that I donate some of that newly acquired money to a worthy cause, such as a favourite charity. Money, after all, is a form of energy and in sharing my good fortune, I would like to think that others may also benefit from it, forming a kind of flow-on effect. Time is also another valuable way of giving thanks, so you might like to donate some of your time.

Finally, keep in mind that spellcrafting is not always the answer to everything. We all need to learn from life's experiences to order to grow and develop as spiritual beings. Successful spellcrafting is a gift, and one that should not be abused.

Some Points about Working Magick

Before you decide to use magick in order to aid your life, it is very important that you are prepared to take full responsibility for whatever consequences may come due to your working. If you are not prepared to take full responsibility, then you should stop now, as magick is not for you.

When performing magick, the following points should be taken into consideration:

- **Clear Intent** of what you need: This is important. You must know exactly what you want, for magick works best in relation to pure emotion. If you truly desire something to happen, you will have a better chance of your magick being successful than if your desire is merely wishful thinking.
- **Choose the Right Timing** for your magical working: If you take into consideration the phases of the moon and the correct corresponding day in relation to your particular need, then you are adding power to your working.
- **Choose Appropriate Items:** It is important that you clearly determine what you want magick to aid you in, then carefully select what you consider to be the most appropriate items in relation for your magical working. Make sure you have everything you need, including matches to light your candles before you start.
- **Avoid Being Distracted:** While working with magick it is very important that you are fully focused on what you are doing. Distractions and interruptions such as the telephone ringing can cause you to lose sight of the intention behind your working. Make sure you are able to complete your magical working without distractions, in private if necessary.
- **Use Your Own Words:** Despite there being a plethora of spell books and web sites offering spells available, I personally recommend that you use these as a guide and then rewrite all or part, adding your own words. Your own input gives more power to your magical working, as well as helps you avoid stumbling across words which you do not understand, or the correct pronunciation.
- **Be Positive and Patient:** This is an extremely important

point. Be positive not only in what you are saying, but also in the fact that your magical working will work. When your magical working has been completed, remain positive. Never doubt your own power or that of your magick. Almost remember to be patient. Magick does not happen overnight – but it does happen, and not always in with the results you may initially desire.

- **Be Realistic:** If you perform a spell to obtain employment yet you spend your days sitting around watching television, then do not expect magick to work. You must be prepared to play your part as well. Analyse your needs and slowly climb the mountain, so to speak, rather than expecting to just appear at the summit.

A Word on Cursing

Recently on social media someone made a comment due to a run of bad health-related issues. They were wondering if they were "cursed". Without having intimate details of other circumstance in their life, should you find yourself in a similar situation, then more than likely, the answer is "No". The Gods of contemporary witchcraft, or the universe in general, do not "curse". If anything, they will bring instances into our lives for us to learn from (i.e., challenges); they do not do things to us.

Without sounding too arrogant (or even ignorant), I doubt if there are any witch or magical practitioners powerful enough to affect an individual's health alone – that is besides your own self. Have we "willed" such instances to appear into our lives? To refresh your memory, you might like to reread the chapter about "Witch Power" and the section on energy following thought.

Consider the following: You are rushing to catch a train and brush passed a man, causing him to drop and break his mobile phone. Angrily, he yells at you: "May you be cursed with bad luck." Are you? These words have been spoken in emotion and intent. You go about your day and your train is late. This causes you to miss your appointment that you have taken the day off work for. You start thinking about the earlier incident, the man's anger, and the curse he yelled at you. The rest of the week more "bad luck" is experienced. You are now convinced that you have been cursed. And you are. Only not by the man, but by yourself. This is because you have allowed the energy to manifest into thought, and then thought into action.

Returning to my earlier comment about me doubting if there is truly any witch or magical practitioner powerful enough to affect an individual's health, I base this belief on the idealism that the underlying aspect of magick is to become more "aware" through the raising of one's energy, vibration, consciousness, or personal power. (Use whatever term appeals best to you). Why would a person continue to focus on egocentric goals relating to the physical realm? This is stuff from Hollywood movies. The more you walk this path and continue building up your relationship with the Gods, you find that you will attract a whole manner of instances to you – the good, the bad and the ugly. Our goal is to release the emotional attachment and stop passing blame. Remember what I said earlier about contemporary witchcraft being a path of self-responsibility? If you find yourself wondering whether you have been cursed then, for the most part, the answer could very well be "yes" – by your own self.

Living a Magical Life

I believe that witches are walkers between the worlds, existing in the liminal spaces between the physical and the dream-like realms. We commune with the Gods and spirits, we understand the lore found within the natural world, and we have the ability to shape and manipulate the energies that surround us, as well as being the catalyst that causes change to occur. With this knowledge comes much responsibility, especially self-responsibility. We must be aware of our impact upon others who share our space and be able to balance reason with intuition without becoming too attached to either.

Through dwelling in these in-between spaces, we are able to gain much knowledge into the scope of ultimate potentials and possibilities. As it states in the Rede of the Wiccae, we need to learn to "speak little, listen much" when it comes to living a magical life in these modern times.

Magick is real. It is alive and breathing just as we are. Its power lives in our ability to properly integrate it into every aspect of your own lives. Walking the path of a witch is not reserved for weekends or sabbats. It is every moment of every day. It does not mean shouting "I am a witch" from the rooftops and swanning around in panne velvet Renaissance inspired or black Gothic clothing. It is a spiritual belief that for some, has religious overtones, that determines how you live your life, your actions, morals, and personal ethics.

It is the insecure who need to keep reaffirming their beliefs to others. If you are confident in your heart then the Gods will leave you without any doubt that this is the correct path for you.

I came across this path in the late 1980s before the internet, social media and indeed a seemingly endless supply of books and courses. In the early 1990s I undertook my first formal instruction and since that time there have been many of occasions when I sought to walk away and have a "normal" life. However, the Craft tends flows through my veins. It determines my personal ethics and morals, and how I perceive things in the world around me.

In this day and age, I feel it is increasingly important to understand the land upon which you reside. Living in Australia, the guardianship of the land for the Aboriginal people is extremely important and is something that I feel often is missing within the West culture. Regardless of what our personal belief is, science has proven that all life began in the oceans before moving onto the land, just like a mother giving birth.

As creations of the land, connecting to the earth strengthens our inner yearning to belong. This can be do through learning about the birds and plants that are both native and introduced to your area. What are their magical or even medicinal properties? Going outside and listening to the sounds, taking in the scents and visions that are around you. Pouring offerings to the spirit of a place can also be undertaken. Even finding out the history of the land upon which you reside. Take a leaf out of the indigenous peoples' book and do not just take from the land -instead actually become part of it, just like your magick.

Appendix

Basic Circle Casting Ritual

There are numerous ways to construct rituals and indeed just as many books and/or internet sites to instruct in the same, some of which are listed at the end of this book. As mentioned earlier, there are eight basic steps when it comes to standard circle casting. The following has been adapted from advice on circle casting which also appears in *Dancing the Sacred Wheel*:

1 **Preparation:** This includes setting up the altar and making sure that it is decorated in a manner that is pleasing to you and that you have everything you need for the ritual including miscellaneous items, such as matches to light the candles. If you do not have an altar or specific ritual tools, that is fine. You should have at least one candle placed in the centre of your working space, as this represents not only deity (spirit) but also the fire element. Check the basic ritual etiquette guideline to ensure that these have been followed.

2 **Purification:** Setting up the area you will be using, you will construct an altar, cleansing the area with incense and salted water. Prior to the ritual some people have a ritual bath, put on special robes or clothing, or spend time meditating on the proposed ritual in order to put you in the right frame of mind for ritual work.

    When you are ready to begin your ritual, light the altar candle, and incense stock or charcoal disk and place it in the censer.

3 **Physical Circle Casting:** This can be either visualising yourself in a bubble of protection, or physically casting a circle around the space you are to work in, usually done in a deosil (anti-clockwise in the Southern Hemisphere or clockwise in the Northern Hemisphere) direction. There

are a number of differing methods to do this, depending on what beliefs you have and what tradition you are following. Some people call upon the ancient elemental guardians to their specific quarters, to help in guarding their sacred space. Others also invite a specific deity or deities into their circle.

Face east and hold your athame (or use your dominant hand with the first two fingers pointing outwards) out before you. Visualise golden light streaming from above into you. Move slowly around your circle in a deosil direction making the circle (east, north, west, south and back to east again in the Southern Hemisphere or east, south, west, north and east in the Northern Hemisphere). As you do this, visualise the golden light projecting out from your athame or finger, forming a circle around you. As you move, state the following or similar words that you prefer. More commonly used, wording can be found in books such as *A Witch's Bible*[52] by Janet and Stewart Farrar or the *Real Witch* series by Kate West, as well as on the internet.

I cast this circle around about
to keep all unwanted spirits out
In the God and Goddess I trust,
this circle I make with perfect love
With the elements four fold,
it is in the fifth that my circle shall hold
I cast this circle with my spirit free,
as my word, so mote it be.

There are many ways to consecrate the working area but the following technique enhances your powers of visualization. Mix some salt into a chalice containing some water and then place your hands above the chalice.

Visualise a bright, golden light hovering above the water. As you say the following words, visualise the light descending into the water, purifying it:

Water and salt when you are cast
No spell nor adverse purpose last
Not in complete accord with me
As my word, so mote it be.[53]

Process around the circle in a deosil direction, asperge your circle by sprinkling the water as you do, visualizing the drops as golden light. When you have finished, replace the chalice upon the altar.

Place your hands around the candle and again visualise the light descending, blending with the candle flame. Say the following words that will turn the candle into a beacon of pure light:

Creature of Fire this charge I lay
No phantom in thy presence stay
Here I will address to thee
As my word, so mote it be.[54]

Take the candle around the circle before setting it back upon the altar.

Finally, place your hands above the incense and say the following words to turn the incense into purifying smoke:

Creature of Air this charge I lay
No phantom in thy presence stay
Here I will address to thee
As my word, so mote it be.[55]

Take the incense around the circle, censing your circle as

you go, before setting it back upon the altar.

4 **Invocation of Elemental Quarters**: The elementals are often called upon to guard the four directions. Face east, raise your arms above your head in an honouring position, and call upon the Guardians of each of the four elements in turn while facing the appropriate direction. You may like to include drawing the appropriate invoking elemental pentagrams. However, if this is done, then the corresponding banishing elemental pentagrams should be used at the end of the ritual. See Appendix C for the invoking elemental pentagrams. There are many forms of elemental calls that you can use. The following are based along the lines of more traditional evocations:

Lords of the Watchtowers of the east
Guardians of air
I ask that you be present and witness my rites.
Be welcome in my circle.

Lords of the Watchtowers of the north
Guardians of fire
I ask that you be present and witness my rites.
Be welcome in my circle.

Lords of the Watchtowers of the west
Guardians of water
I ask that you be present and witness my rites.
Be welcome in my circle.

Lords of the Watchtowers of the south
Guardians of earth
I ask that you be present and witness my rites.
Be welcome in my circle.

5 **Invocation of Deity**: Calling into your circle the chosen deity or deities that you wish to work with during the ritual. If you do not have any specific deity in mind, then more generic terms such as God and Goddess can be used.

God and Goddess, my Lord and Lady
I build this circle as a place that is sacred in your honour
I ask you to be present here with me tonight
To fill my circle and my heart with your love and you.
Be welcome in my circle.

6 **Main Body of the Ritual**: This is where you carry out what you have set up your sacred space to do – craft spells or magick, meditate to gain information or communicate with the Gods. You may wish to state the purpose of the ritual, as in doing this, you avoid creating havoc or losing focus on what you are supposed to be working towards. If you are to undertake spellcrafting or do some healing then you should choose a method by which you will raise your cone of power.

7 **Offering and Libation**: This is often performed during esbats and sabbats where offerings of food and drink are blessed and made to the Gods as opposed to during other more general magical workings.

8 **Opening Your Circle**: Acknowledging the presence of the Gods and giving thanks for their attendance. This should come from your heart. An example of thanking the Gods is:

God and Goddess, Lord and Lady
I thank you for attending my rite
And for bestowing upon me your wisdom and compassion.

Until we meet again, blessed be.

Then dismiss each of the elemental guardians, starting in the south (north for the Northern Hemisphere) and moving in a widdershins direction back around the circle until you come back to east. If you have used the invoking elemental pentagrams when you called the Guardians into your circle, then you need to use the banishing pentagrams in order to dismiss them properly at the end of your ritual. An example of the wording is as follows:

Lords of the Watchtowers of the south
Guardians of earth
I thank you for your presence in my rite.
And I bid you hail and farewell.

Lords of the Watchtowers of the west
Guardians of water
I thank you for your presence in my rite.
And I bid you hail and farewell.

Lords of the Watchtowers of the north
Guardians of fire
I thank you for your presence in my rite.
And I bid you hail and farewell.

Lords of the Watchtowers of the east
Guardians of air
I thank you for your presence in my rite.
And I bid you hail and farewell.

As you retrace your steps, visualise the circle disappearing back into your athame (or finger). Then declare that the ritual is completed and the circle open. The ringing of a bell or clapping of hands helps dispense any lingering energetic residue. Make sure the all candles are extinguished (use a candle snuffer or your fingers – never blow out a candle that you have used in ritual) unless you are wanting them to burn out by themselves. If the latter, then ensure you place them in a safe spot. If you have used charcoal disks, these should be left until the following morning before being disposed of in the rubbish.

Any libations of the wine or juice that you have made, as well as cakes/biscuits should be taken outside and placed in the garden. If you do not have a garden, then you might wish to take a walk to your local community garden or park, and discreetly dispose of your offerings there.

Elemental Pentagrams

Invoking Pentagram of Air

Banishing Pentagram of Air

Invoking Pentagram of Earth

Banishing Pentagram of Earth

Invoking Pentagram of Fire

Banishing Pentagram of Fire

Invoking Pentagram of Water

Banishing Pentagram of Water

Self-Blessing/ Dedication Ritual

If you decide that contemporary witchcraft is a path that resonates with you, then you might like to formally dedicate yourself to it, noting that initiation generally only occurs in a coven format. The following ritual can be used as a template, allowing you to adapt it to your needs, or you may like to follow it as it is. It can be performed skyclad (naked) or robed depending in how comfortable you feel.

Before you undertake this ritual, you might like to make some notes in your magical diary about why you want to dedicate yourself to this path, what this means to you. You might even like to rewrite part of the following in order to personalise the ritual to include aspects that are meaningful to you.

Ensure that you have the following items:

- Blessing Oil (this can be a base oil with a few drops of essential oil added)
- A white candle (or a hand rolled beeswax candle)

Begin by grounding yourself through the Four-Fold Breath. Following the format as set out in "Basic Circle Casting", begin by casting your circle. At number 6 (the main body of the ritual) pause and light your candle. As you focus on the candle flame, considering what goals you have for yourself on your spiritual journey. Visualise drawing the warmth of the flame into your heart (*anahata*). Think about your motivations for performing this self-dedication, and then say:

I, [your name], *have prepared myself for dedication to the path of the ancient Gods.*
I am a child of the Gods and desire to walk with them.
I ask that they bestow upon me wisdom and compassion, integrity

and discretion,
and the strength to always work in accordance with my True Will.
So mote it be.

Dip your finger into the Blessing Oil, and with eyes closed, anoint your forehead. You can anoint yourself with a pentagram, cross, circle or any other symbol that has personal significance to you. Say:

Blessed be my mind that holds the flame of curiosity and serves as a beacon for light.
May I always be open to receive the wisdom of the Gods.

You are now to anoint other parts of your body. Some people anoint the lips, breasts, phallus/womb (above the line of the pubic hair), knees and feet. Others anoint the seven chakra areas (top of head, third eye, throat, heart, solar plexus, sacral and above the line of the pubic hair). A more traditional self-blessing is

Carefully anoint the eyelids and say:

Blessed be my eyes that know the magick of finding the beauty in everyone they see.
May I always see my way clearly upon this path.

Anoint your throat, and say:

Blessed be my voice that utters the sacred names
May I always speaks my truth in tones of honour, power and self-possession

Anoint your chest, and say:

Blessed be my heart that that is whole and lacking in nothing, able

to abide fully in love.
May I always love and be loved.

Anoint the palms of each of your hands, and say:

Blessed be my hands that create beauty in the world and carry the
weight of this life with such strength and courage.
May I use them to help others.

Anoint your genital area, and say (use the term more appropriate
for you):

Blessed be my womb/phallus that connects me to the life pulse of
all things.
May I honour the creation of life.

Anoint your knees, and say:

Blessed be my knees, so that I may kneel at the sacred altar.
May I always remain humble as I progress along this path.

Anoint the soles of your feet, and say:

Blessed be my feet that carries be along this sacred path.
May I always be grateful for the lessons I receive.

If you are drawn to a specific deity, you can now pledge your
devotion and dedication to them. Otherwise, using the generic
"God and Goddess" or "Lord and Lady" is equally appropriate.
If the following does not resonate with you, then you can write
your own dedication:

Tonight, I pledge my dedication to the God and Goddess.
I will walk with them beside me, and ask them to guide me on this

journey.

I pledge to honour them, and ask that they allow me to grow closer to them.

As I will, so mote it be.

Take some time to meditate. Feel the afterglow of what you have done and the energy of the Gods around you as you have brought yourself to their attention.

When you are ready, continue with the ritual format. You might like to make a libation and toast yourself before opening your circle. Make sure that you record your ritual in your magical diary.

Cleansing Salt Scrub and Ritual Oil

Within my initial training into contemporary witchcraft we were encouraged as much as possible to make our own materials and not to rely on store bought items. Then again, this was the early 1990s and the internet had yet to change the face of the shopping. Despite today's abundance of online stores, I still find it extremely satisfying to make my own products for my ritual practices, such as the recipes for the two products that I share here.

Cleansing Salt Scrub

This salt scrub not only helps to exfoliate your skin by removing dead skin cells, but also removes negative energies and leaves your skin softer and smoother. Simply pour about ½ cup of sea salt into a small container. Add to this just enough extra virgin olive oil to soak the salt and let soak for one minute. Stir the mixture and add more olive oil if needed. The ideal consistency is that of a frozen slushie. Squeeze in the juice of about half a lemon and stir the mixture thoroughly. You can add a few drops of an essential oil if you like however this is not necessary.

Using a wash cloth, loofah, or your bare hand, rub the mixture onto your skin when you take a shower. The salt acts as an exfoliate, the oil as a moisturizer and the lemon as a cleanser.

Simple Ritual Oil

This simple ritual oil can be used to anoint your third eye (ajna chakra) as well as pulse points such as wrists and behind the ears. If you have skin sensitivities, it is always recommended that you do a skin test first to see if you develop a reaction within 24 hours. If you do, then you may wish to simply use the oil on its own (olive oil is sacred to the Greek Goddess Athena), use a further diluted mixture or investigate using scented water.

Into two tablespoons of a carrier or base oil (extra virgin olive oil, safflower, grape seed, jojoba or apricot kernel oil), measure five drops sandalwood essential oil, two drops camphor essential oil and one drop each of orange and patchouli essential oils. Blend well. Pour into in a dark coloured glass bottle and store in a cool, dark place.

Other ritual oils can be purchased through stores such as LunaNoire Creations etsy store[57].

Releasing the Power of the Witch Rite

Paul Huson[58] directs the witch to light a single candle before going to bed on three consecutive nights while visualising chains around the wrists and ankles being struck by bolts of lightning. The witch reads the Lord's Prayer backwards, while visualising chains fall to the ground in molten shards, and all the Judeo-Christian influence being lifted from the proverbial shoulders.

I have personally found it useful to undertake this ritual at least once a year as part of the process of self-examination. If I feel restricted or emotionally undone, that I have found that using this rite can bring to the surface any underlying issues to be dealt with. This is certainly true if the problem is one stemming from Judeo-Christian indoctrination and sometimes this can only be discovered through performance of the ritual.

The rite is most effective when incorporated to a ritual format. If you are using the basic ritual provided in this book, then Releasing the Power of the Witch can be inserted at step 6.

Nema! Livee, morf su revilled tub noishaytpmet ootni ton suh deel sus tshaiga sapsert taht yeth. Vigrawf derb ilaid rua yed sith suh vig neveh ni si za thre ni nud eeb liw eyth muck modngik eyth main eyth eeb dwohlah nevah ni tra chioo.
Reth art rua!
[Note: text is written phonetically.]

After the rite, sit quietly and observe what comes to the surface of your consciousness. If a destructive pattern, or whatever, is identified, you may wish to write it down on a piece of paper which is then burnt. Ensure that your record in detail what you have done and what is observed in your magical diary.

Making Your Own Robe

According to the Servants of the Light[59] (a Western esoteric order), making your own robe is a relatively simple process, even if you have no sewing skills. All you need is a piece of material that is 150 cm wide and at least twice your length (from shoulder to floor) plus a few extra centimetres. While the colour is entirely up to you, the preferred fabric should be something natural, i.e., cotton or linen, or even a blend of these.

Fold the material in half (A), making it slightly taller than your shoulder height: Fold it a second time lengthwise (B) resulting in four levels of cloth as tall as your shoulder height and about 75 cm wide. Make a hole for the neck by cutting out a small quarter-circle in the corner where the folds meet:

Put a pin (C) at the left edge, about 35 cm from the top edge, and a second pin (D) 30 cm from the top edge. Add 25 cm to your chest/bust measurement then divide by four. Put a third pin (E) this distance to the left of the pin at (D).

Draw a line on the cloth from (C) to (E). Put a fourth pin (F) along

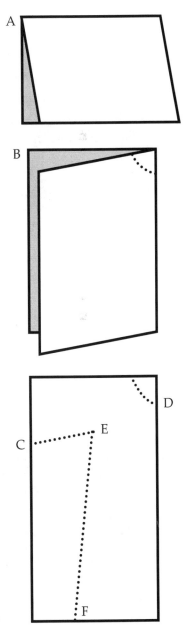

the bottom edge, about 45-50 cm from the right edge (double join). Draw a line from this pin to (E). Remove the pins and cut through all four layers of cloth along the line from (C) to (E) and then to (F).

Unfold the material along the right edge (double join) and you should have a "T" shape.

Turn inside out and sew along the line (C) to (E) to (F) on both sides. Sew the neckline, making a vertical cut along the middle large enough to get your head through. Put your robe on and adjust the length using some pins. Sew along the hem line, remove the pins – and your robe is ready to wear.

There should also be enough material left over to make a hood for your robe if you wish.

Glossary

The following are some terms used within contemporary witchcraft:

Akasha: The spiritual ether (or aether). The omnipresent fifth element that embraces the other four (earth, air, fire and water) and from which they stem. This is the realm of "pattern" or causality, from which the realm the normally thought of five senses manifests.

Altar: A special, flat surface set aside exclusively for magical workings or religious acknowledgment.

Amulet: A magically-charged object which deflects specific, usually negative energies. A protective object.

Animism: A belief of there being a living soul found in plants, inanimate objects and natural phenomena.

Asperge: To flick salt water around the circle as a means of cleansing it with elements of water and earth.

Astral Plane: A place which is generally conceptualized as an invisible parallel world which remains unseen from our own solid world of form.

Bane/Baneful: That which destroys life, which is poisonous, dangerous or even destructive.

Banish: To magically end something or exorcise unwanted entities. To rid the presence of.

Bealtaine: Ritual observance marking the gateway to summer.

Bind: To magically restrain something or someone.

Blessed Be: A term of greeting and parting.

Burning Times: A term used to describe the period of persecution in the Middle Ages and later of witches, pagans, Jews and heretics of the Catholic Church. Not all people who were condemned of witchcraft by the Church were witches, and not all were burned. In England they were hung.

Blue Moon: Whenever there are two full moons in one calendar month, the second is referred to as a blue moon.

Book of Shadows: A hand-copied book containing rituals, recipes, training techniques, guidelines, and other materials considered important to a witch or a coven.

Charging: To infuse an object with personal power.

Cleansing: Removing negative energies, vibrations or images from an object or space by utilising positive, psychic energy.

Cone of Power: The ritual act of raising energy in the form of a spiral light and then directing it towards a specific goal.

Consecration: The act, process or ceremony of making something sacred; to remove negative or unwanted energies.

Conscious Mind: The analytical, materially-based, rational half of our consciousness. The part of our mind that is at work while we communicate and perform acts related to the physical world.

Consecration: The act of blessing an object or place by instilling it with positive energy.

Correspondence: An item that has a magical association with other items. Correspondences include: days, planets, moon phases, herbs, oils, colours, gemstones, astrological signs, hours, etc.

Dedication: The process where a person accepts the Craft as their path and vows to study and learn all that is necessary to reach initiation. It is a conscious preparation to accept something new into your life and stick with it, regardless of the highs and lows that may follow.

Degree: A system marking the progress of the witch within contemporary witchcraft. First Degree usually denotes a person who has entered the priesthood and is training to understand the mysteries contained within contemporary witchcraft. Second Degree is someone who has understood some of the mysteries, therefore allowing them to offer some teaching to others. Third Degree is someone who has fully understood the mysteries and therefore can ultimately perform initiations and start their own coven.

Deosil: Meaning "with the sun", the most common direction in which a circle is cast. Symbolic of life, positive magick and positive energies.

Drawing Down the Moon: A ritual performed during the full moon by witches to empower themselves and unite their essence with a particular deity, usually the Goddess.

Drawing Down the Sun: Lesser-known and used companion ritual to Drawing Down the Moon in which the essence of the Sun God is drawn into the body of a male witch.

Elements: Four essences that are the building blocks of the universe: earth, air, fire and water.

Esbat: A gathering or ritual usually occurring on the full moon and dedicated to the Goddess in her lunar aspect.

Evocation: Used in religious ceremonies and magical rites. An invitation of or summoning forth of an entity or deity to be present usually to appear to witness the rites and protect the circle.

Familiar: A magical equal, usually an animal partner that shows unusual psychic intelligence with its human counterpart. Not necessarily a pet.

Grounding: To disperse excess energy generated during magical works by sending it into the earth. A process of centring one's self back in the physical world.

Handfasting: A betrothal ceremony in which the hands of each party are tied together with a consecrated knot to signify the union. There are three basic lengths: a year and a day, a lifetime, and for all eternity.

Higher Self: That part of us which connects our corporeal minds to the collective unconscious and with the divine knowledge of the universe.

Imbolc: Ritual observance marking the gateway to spring, first spring festival.

Immanent: Existing or operating with; deity permanently pervading and sustaining the universe.

Initiation: A ceremony marking entry into the mysteries contained within contemporary witchcraft through the three-degree system. Not to be confused with dedication.

Invocation: An invitation to an entity or deity to be present usually enter into the physical body of the person.

Litha: An alternative name for the summer solstice originally coined by American author Aidan Kelly that has no actual historical evidence let alone there being any such deity.

Lughnasadh: Ritual observance marking the gateway to autumn, first harvest festival, associated with the grain. Also known as "Lammas".

Mabon: A character from Welsh mythology associated with the sun. American author Aidan Kelly started using this word as an alternate name for the autumn equinox in the early 1990s despite there being no connection with the equinox.

Macrocosm: The world around us. The cosmos as a whole, in relation to the microcosm, its detailed manifestation (the human being in particular). In accordance with the Hermetic principle "as above, so below", the microcosm is of the same essence as the macrocosm and reflects its nature.

Magick: The projection of natural energies (such as personal power) to bring about needed change. Magick is the process of raising this energy, giving it purpose, and releasing it.

Microcosm: The world within us. Detailed manifestation in the whole plan of things, the human being's place in the cosmos (macrocosm).

Monotheism: Belief in one supreme deity who has no other forms or who displays no other aspects.

Neophyte: A seeker or newcomer to magical practices.

Omnipresent: Concept of divinity's presence being everywhere simultaneously.

Pantheon: A collection or group of Gods in a particular religious or mythical structure.

Pantheism: Belief in many deities who are really one because they are all merely aspects of the single creative life source. Paganism is pantheistic.

Pentacle: A star within a circle, or a similar object used in magick. One of the four elemental tools, an engraved disc representing the element of earth. It is normally the centre piece of an altar.

Pentagram: An equilateral five-pointed star. An upright pentagram (with the single point upwards) represents the four elements governed by the fifth, spirit. A symbol of power and protection.

Polytheism: Belief in the existence of many unrelated deities each with their own dominion and interests who have no spiritual or familial relationships to one another.

Projective Hand: The hand thought to be the point through which personal power is sent from the body.

Psychic Mind: The subconscious or unconscious mind, in which we receive psychic impressions. It is at work when we sleep, dream, and meditate.

Qabalah: Mystical teaching from the Jewish-Gnostic tradition used within ceremonial magick and the Alexandrian tradition. The Tree of Life glyph forms a model for the creation of the microcosm through the progressive descent of divine energy through various spheres (parts of the human psyche) to the microcosm.

Receptive Hand: The hand through which energy is received, opposite to the projective hand.

Sabbat: A witch's festival relating to the seasons.

Samhain: Ritual observance marking the gateway to winter, third harvest festival, associated with the culling of animals.

Sky Clad: Being naked, while performing a magical ritual or act. Considered to be deeply spiritual and not at all sexual.

Subconscious Mind: Part of the mind which functions below the

· levels we are able to access in the course of a normal working day.

Sympathetic Magic: Concept of like attracting like. The most common way spells are worked.

Talisman: An object charged with personal power designed to attract a specific force or energy to its bearer.

Transcendent: Beyond or above the range of normal or physical human experience.

Tutelary: A protector, guardian or spirit of a special place.

Warlock: Oath-breaker or liar. Often incorrectly used in reference to a male witch.

Watchtowers: The four cardinal points, regarded as guardians of the magick circle and which are represented by the four elementals.

Widdershins: "Against the sun", used for Underworld working, banishing, dispersing energies or even negative magical purposes.

About the Author

Frances Billinghurst has been a student of metaphysics, Goddess spirituality and the occult arts for most of her adult life. An initiate of a traditional style of contemporary witchcraft who founded the Temple of the Dark Moon in 1999, Frances is also a practicing occultist and budding mythologist as well as an esoteric lecturer.

In 2003, Frances led the opening ritual of the New Zealand Pagan Fest with Chief Druid Philip Carr-Gomm, and in 2010, she was accompanied by occult philosopher Ramsay Dukes. She has also presented lectures at the Australia Wiccan Conference, the Australian Goddess Conference, worked with renowned Wiccan elders Janet Farrar and Gavin Bone, and held the position of secretary for the Pagan Alliance Incorporated (South Australia) for six consecutive years.

Aside from running an active coven, Frances is the author of *Encountering the Dark Goddess: A Journey into the Shadow Realms, Dancing the Sacred Wheel: A Journey through the Southern Sabbats* and *In Her Sacred Name: Writings about the Divine Feminine,* and editor of *Call of the God: An Anthology exploring the Divine Masculine within Modern Paganism.* A prolific writer Frances has had articles appear in over 20 publications, including the Llewellyn *Witch's Calendar, The Cauldron* and *Circle,* as well as being a regular columnist for Australia's No.1 spiritual lifestyle magazine, *Insight,* for 10 years. Her essays and poetry can also be found in numerous anthologies including *Unto Herself: A Devotional Anthology for Independent Goddess* (edited by Ashley Horne and Bibliotheca Alexandrina), *The Faerie Queens* (edited by Sorita d'Este and David Rankine), *Queen of Olympos: A Devotional Anthology to Hera and Iuno* (edited by Lykeia and Bibliotheca Alexandrina), *A Mantle of Stars: A Devotional Anthology to the Queen of Heaven* (edited by Jen Connelly and Bibliotheca

Alexandrina), and *Blood, Bone and Blade: A Tribute to the Morrigan* (edited by Nicole Ross and Bibliotheca Alexandrina).

When she is not attempting to turn her patch of parched Australian dirt into something that slightly resembles the Hanging Gardens of Babylon, Frances also crafts an assortment of beaded jewellery and crystal mala beads, as well as devotional beads. These items are available for purchase through LunaNoire Creations - https://www.etsy.com/au/shop/LunaNoireCreations.

Endnotes

1. Guiley, Rosemary Ellen, "Canon Episcopi", *The Encyclopaedia of Witches and Witchcraft* (Facts on File, 1989)

2. Behringer, Wolfgang, *Witches and Witch Hunts: A Global History* (Polity, 2004)

3. Gardner, Gerald, *The Meaning of Witchcraft* (Weiser Books, 2004)

4. Jones, June, *King of the Witches: The World of Alex Sanders* (C. Davies, 1969)

5. Crowley, Vivianne, *Wicca: Old Religion for a New Age* (Thorsons, 1992)

6. Beckett, John "An Authentic Foundation for Modern Paganism", retrieved from https://www.patheos.com/blogs/johnbeckett/2019/12/an-authentic-foundation-for-modern-paganism.html

7. Seims, Melissa, "Wica or Wicca? Politics and the Power of Words", retrieved from http://www.thewica.co.uk/ wica_or_wicca.htm

8. Crowley, Aleister, *Liber AL vel Legis: The Book of the Law* (Red Wheel/ Weiser, 1987)

9. Kraus, Lawrence M., *A Universe from Nothing: Why There Is Something Rather Than Nothing* (Atria Books, 2012)

10. The concept of "Will" is explained in more detail in a later section.

11. In his biography, *Memory, Dreams, Reflections*, psychoanalyst Carl Jung records his personal encounters with the "psychic reality" of the archetypes, concluding that they are real. For the witch, archetypes are psychic vehicles that are perceived through the consciousness but also inhabit the unconscious.

12. Bibleinfo.com, "When was Jesus born?", retrieved from www.bibleinfo.com

13. Eliade, Mircea, *Shamanism: Archaic Techniques of Ecstasy* (HarperCollins, 1997)

14. D'Este, Sorita and Rankine, David, *Wicca Magical Beginnings - A Study of the Possible Origins of the Rituals and Practices Found in This Modern Tradition of Pagan Witchcraft and Magick* (Avalonia, 2008)

15. Online version retrieved from http://www.krishna.com/ bhagavad-gita-online-versions

16. Fitch, Ed, *A Grimoire of Shadows: Witchcraft, Paganism, and Magick* (Llewellyn Publications, 1996)

17. Cunningham, Scott, *Wicca: A Guide for the Solitary Practitioner* (Llewellyn Publications, 1989)

18. MacMorgan, Kaatryn, *Wicca 333: Advanced Topics in Wiccan Belief* (iUniverse Inc, 2003)

19. ibid

20. Mooney, Thorn, "Traditional Wicca in the American South", retrieved from https://thornthewitch.wordpress.com

21. Cochrane, Robert, 1964, "The Craft Today", *Pentagram Magazine*, retrieved from "Clan of Tubal Cain", http://www. clanoftubalcain.org.uk/the_letters /TCT_article_lk.pdf

22. Huson, Paul, *Mastering Witchcraft: A Practical Guide for Witches, Warlocks and Covens* (Perigee Trade, 1987)

23. Walker, Barbara, *The Woman's Encyclopaedia of Myths and Secrets* (HarperOne, 1983)

24. Gray, William G, *Inner Traditions of Magic* (Weiser, 1970)

25. ibid

26. Butler, W.E., *The Magician, His Training and His Work* (Aquarian Paperback, 1982)

27. Fortune, Dion, *Applied Magic and Aspects of Occultism* (Thoth Publications, 1995)

28. Starhawk, *The Spiral Dance: A Rebirth of the Ancient Religion of the Great Goddess* (Harper & Collins, 1979)

29. Gardner, Gerald, "The Magical Legend of the Witches", retrieved https://www.sacred-texts.com/bos/bos350.htm

30. Nightmare, M Macha, "The Mighty Dead, the Beloved Dead and Us" (2001), retrieved from http://www.witchvox. com/va/dt_va.html?a=usca&c= holidays&id=3673

31. Billinghurst, Frances, *Dancing the Sacred Wheel* (TDM Publishing, 2014)

32. ibid

33. One web site that provides such information is Archaeoastronomy (http://www.archaeo astronomy.com/index.html)

34. The somewhat modern belief that Samhain is the "Celtic new year" is historically incorrect and one that I explain about in *Dancing the Sacred Wheel*. Likewise, the incorrect association with Samhain being the "witch's new year". While I am not sure when such erroneous information entered the teachings of modern Wicca, it does not form part of contemporary witchcraft.

35. Greer, John Michael, *The New Encyclopaedia of the Occult* (Llewelyn Publications, 2003)

36. Merriam Webster online dictionary, retrieved from https://www.merriam-webster.com/dictionary/meditate

37. LunaNoire Creations online etsy store: https://www.etsy.com/au/shop/ LunaNoireCreations where custom beading orders are welcome.

38. Rankine, David, *Becoming Magick* (Mandrake, 2004)

39. Rowe, Benjamin, "The Essential Skills of Magic", retrieved from https://hermetic.com /norton/pentagram_ritual

40. Cabot, Laurie and Cowan, Thomas, *Power of the Witch: The Earth, the Moon and the Magical Path to Enlightenment* (Arkana, 1992)

41. Gardner, Gerald, *The Gardnerian Book of Shadows* (1957), Retrieved from https://www.sacred-texts.com/pag/ gbos/gbos32.htm

42. Tyson, Donald, *New Millennium Magic: A Complete System of Self Realization* (Llewellyn Publications, 1996)

43. Gardner, Gerald (1953), "Power" from *The Gardnerian Book of Shadows*, (retrieved from Sacred Texts, https://www.sacred-texts.com/pag/gbos /gbos19.htm)

44. Fortune, Dion, *Psychic Self Defence* (Weiser Books, 2001)

45. Franklin, Anna, *Pagan Ritual* (Lear Books, 2008)

46. Lévi, Eliphas, *Transcendental Magic: Its Doctrine and Ritual* (Weiser Books, 2011)

47. Lévi, Eliphas, *The Great Secret: Or Occultism Unveiled* (Weiser Books, 2000)

48. Bell, Jessie Wicker (Lady Sheba), *The Grimoire of Lady Sheba* (Llewellyn Publications, 2001)

49. Billinghurst, Frances, *On Her Silver Rays: Moon, Magic and Myth of the Queen the of Heavens and the Starry Skies* (TBA)

50. Aboriginal Indigenous Astronomy, retrieved from http://www.aboriginal astronomy.com.au/content/topics/moon/

51. Rinpoche, Sogyal, *The Tibetan Book of Living and Dying* (Harper San Francesco, 1994)

52. Farrar, Janet and Stewart, *A Witch's Bible: A Complete Witch's Handbook* (Phoenix Publishing, 1996)

53. Huson, Paul, *Mastering Witchcraft: A Practical Guide for Witches, Warlocks and Covens* (Perigee Trade, 1987)

54. ibid

55. ibid

56. To "evoke" means to call something forth, i.e., calling an elemental, spirit, or deity into the sacred space that you have created. To "invoke", on the other hand, means to call a spirit or deity into your physical self, as in a form of possession or channelling, i.e. when a High Priestess draws down the moon, which is a form of invocation.

57. LunaNoire Creations online etsy store can be found here: https://www.etsy. com /au/shop/LunaNoireCreations where custom beading orders are welcome.

58. Huson, Paul, 1987, *Mastering Witchcraft: A Practical Guide for Witches, Warlocks and Covens* (Perigee Trade)

59. Servants of the Light, "Making a Robe", retrieved from https://www.servants ofthelight.org/knowledge/making-a-robe

Bibliography

Many books have found their way onto my library shelves. The following are a few that I consider to be worth reading for the neophyte interested in contemporary witchcraft and its influences:

Alder, Margot, *Drawing down the Moon* (Beacon Press, 1984)

Bardon, Franz, *Initiation into Hermetics: The Path of the True Adept* (Merkur Publishing, 199)

Bell, Jessica Wicker (Lady Sheba), *Lady Sheba's Book of Shadows* (Llewellyn Publications, 2002)

Beyerl, Paul, *The Master Book of Herbalism* (Phoenix Publishing, 1994)

— , *A Compendium of Herbal Magick* (Phoenix Publishing, 1998)

Billinghurst, Frances, *Dancing the Sacred Wheel: A Journey through the Southern Sabbats* (TDM Publishing, 2014)

Buckland, Raymond, *Buckland's Complete Book of Witchcraft* (Llewellyn Publications, 1986)

Cicero, Chic and Cicero, Sandra Tabatha, *The Essential Golden Dawn* (Llewellyn Publications, 2003)

Cochrane, Robert, *The Robert Cochrane Letters: An Insight into Modern Traditional Witchcraft* (Capall Bann Publishing, 2003)

Crowther, Patricia, *Covensense* (Robert Hale Ltd, 2009)

Crowley, Vivianne, *Wicca: Old Religion for a New Age* (Thorsons, 1992)

Cunningham, Scott, *Incense, Oils and Brews* (Llewellyn Publications, 1988)

—, *Cunningham's Encyclopedia of Magical Herbs* (Llewellyn Publications, 1985)

D'este, Sorita and Rankine, David, *Wicca Magical Beginnings - A Study of the Possible Origins of the Rituals and Practices Found in This Modern Tradition of Pagan Witchcraft and Magick* (Avalonia,

2008)

Farrar, Janet and Stewart, *A Witch's Bible: A Complete Witch's Handbook* (Phoenix Publishing, 1996)

Franklin, Anna, *The Hearth Witch's Compendium: Magical and Natural Living for Every Day* (Llewellyn Publishing, 2017)

Frazer, James, *The Golden Bough: A Study in Magic and Religion: A New Abridgement from the Second and Third Editions* (Oxford World's Classics, 2009)

Gardner, Gerald, *The Meaning of Witchcraft* (Weiser Books, 2004)
—, *Witchcraft Today* (Magical Childe Publishing Inc, 1991)

Gary, Gemma, *Traditional Witchcraft: A Cornish Book of Ways* (Troy Books, 2008)

Ginzberg, Carlos, *The Night Battles: Witchcraft & Agrarian Cults in the Sixteenth & Seventeenth Centuries* (Johns Hopkins University Press, 1992)

Ginzberg, Carlos, and Rosenthal, Raymond, *Ecstasies: Deciphering the Witches' Sabbath* (University of Chicago Press, 2004

Glass, Justine, *Witchcraft, the Sixth Sense and Us* (Neville Spearman, 1965)

Graves, Robert, *The White Goddess: A Historical Grammar of Poetic Myth* (Faber & Faber, 1999)

Green, Marion, *A Witch Alone: Thirteen Moons to Master Natural Magic* (Aquarian Press, 1991)

Guiley, Rosemary Ellen, *The Encyclopaedia of Witches and Witchcraft* (Facts on File, 1999)

Heselton, Philip, *Wiccan Roots: Gerald Gardner and the Modern Witchcraft Revival* (Capall Bann Publishing, 2000)
—, *Witchfather: A Life of Gerald Gardner: Volume 1, Into the Witch Cult* (Thoth Publications, 2012)
—, *Witchfather: A Life of Gerald Gardner: Volume 2, From Witch Cult to Wicca* (Thoth Publications, 2012)
—, *Doreen Valiente: Witch* (Centre for Pagan Studies, 2016)

Howard, Michael, *Modern Wicca: A History from Gerald Gardner to the Present* (Llewellyn Publications, 2010)

—, *Children of Cain: A Study of Modern Traditional Witchcraft* (Three Hands Press, 2011)

—, *Liber Nox: A Traditional Witch's Gramarye* (Skylight Press, 2014)

Hume, Lynne, *Witchcraft and Paganism in Australia* (Melbourne University, 1997)

Huson, Paul, *Mastering Witchcraft: A Practical Guide for Witches, Warlocks and Covens* (Perigee Trade, 1987)

Hutton, Ronald, *The Triumph of the Moon: A History of Modern Pagan Witchcraft* (Oxford University Press, 2001)

—, *The Witch: A History of Fear, from Ancient Times to the Present* (Yale University Press, 2018)

Jackson, Nigel Aldcroft, *Call of the Horned Piper* (Capall Bann Publishing, 2001)

—, *Masks of Misrule: The Horned God and His Cult in Europe* (Capall Bann Publishing, 1996)

John of Monmouth, *Genuine Witchcraft is Explained: The Secret History of the Royal Windsor Coven and the Regency* (Capall Bann Publishing; 2012)

Jones, Evan John and Valiente, Doreen, *The Roebuck in the Thicket: An Anthology of the Robert Cochrane Witchcraft Tradition* (Capall Bann Publishing, 2002)

Kraig, Donald Michael, *Modern Magick Eleven Lessons in the High Magical Arts* (Llewellyn Publications, 1988)

Leland, Charles, *Aradia: Gospel of the Witches* (Phoenix Publishing, 1998)

Murray, Margaret, *The Witch-Cult in Western Europe: A Study in Anthropology* (

—, *The God of the Witches* (Oxford University Press, 1970)

Pearson, Nigel, *Treading the Mill: Practical Craft Working in Modern Traditional Witchcraft* (Capall Bann Publishing, 2007)

Rainbird, Ariadne, and Rankine, David, *Magick without Peers* (Capall Bann Publishing, 1998)

Sanders, Maxine, *Firechild* (Mandrake Publications, 2007)

Starhawk,, *The Spiral Dance: A Rebirth of the Ancient Religion of the Great Goddess* (HarperCollins Publishers, 1989)

—, *The Pagan Book of Living and Dying: Practical Rituals, Prayers, Blessings, and Meditations on Crossing Over* (HarperCollins Publishers, 1997)

Valiente, Doreen, *An ABC of Witchcraft Past and Present* (St Martin's Press, 1978)

—, *Witchcraft for Tomorrow* (Phoenix Publishing Inc, 1987)

—, *The Rebirth of Witchcraft* (Phoenix Publishing Inc, 1989)

Index

Alexandrian 15, 19, 20, 22, 43
Ancestors 73, 77, 81-83, 98
Archetypes 75, 76
Athame 147, 155, 157, 158
Autumn Equinox 90, 91, 96, 97

Bealtaine 55, 89, 90, 91, 94
Bell 146, 160
Beltane see Bealtaine
Besom 160
Boline 160
Book of Mirrors 101
Book of Shadows 18, 36, 101, 119, 206
Buckland, Raymond 7, 21, 172
Burning Times 9

Cauldron 160
Chalice 149, 155-158
Cone of Power 173
Cords 160
Crowley, Aleister 10, 12, 23, 25, 26, 36, 60, 116
Cursing 209

Dark Quarter 142
Deosil 86, 131, 132, 167, 174

Egregore 82, 166
Elementals 152, 153

Energy, personal 58, 141, 202
Esbat 20, 29, 158, 166, 170, 186, 219

Farrar, Stewart and Janet 14, 83
Fitch, Ed 37

Gardner, Gerald 1, 2, 9-15, 18-20, 25, 30, 38, 53, 69. 82, 83, 119-122, 129, 155, 155
Gardnerian 7, 19, 20, 22, 50
Gnome 151, 153

Imbolc 89-92

Karma 30, 38, 39, 44, 45

Lammas 95, 96
Law of Cause and Effect 37, 38
Litha see Summer Solstice
Lughnasadh 89, 90, 91, 95, 96

Mabon 98
Mid Summer see Summer Solstice
Mid Winter see Winter Solstice
Mighty Dead 82, 83

Oimelc see Imbolc

Ostara *see* Spring Equinox

Pentacle 150, 154-156, 158,
    159, 161
Pentagram 159, 161-163, 222,
    223
Protection 128, 133, 159, 160,
    163, 169, 183, 185, 186, 190,
    191, 193, 197, 198

Rede of the Wiccae 35, 49, 52

Sabbats 29, 84, 89-91, 132, 158,
    170, 219
Sabbats, Greater 29, 89, 90
Sabbats, Lesser 29, 89
Salamander 147, 152, 153
Samhain 89-91, 97, 98, 132
Sanders, Alex 1, 13, 14, 18, 20,
    83
Scourge 160
Spring Equinox 90, 93
Stang 161

Summer Solstice 90, 95
Sylphs 152, 153

Threefold Law of Return 38,
    39, 40, 61
True Will 36, 40, 41, 50, 58,
    60-62, 129

Undines 149, 153

Valiente, Doreen 12, 35, 51,
    83, 174

Wand 146, 155, 156
Wheel of the Year 29, 44, 46,
    80, 85, 89-91, 152
Wiccan Rede 35, 35, 37, 39,
    49-52, 62, 205
Widdershins 86, 131, 132
Winter Solstice 90-92, 132
Witch Power 117, 209

Yule 56, 91, 92

**MOON
BOOKS**

PAGANISM & SHAMANISM

What is Paganism? A religion, a spirituality, an alternative belief system, nature worship? You can find support for all these definitions (and many more) in dictionaries, encyclopaedias, and text books of religion, but subscribe to any one and the truth will evade you. Above all Paganism is a creative pursuit, an encounter with reality, an exploration of meaning and an expression of the soul. Druids, Heathens, Wiccans and others, all contribute their insights and literary riches to the Pagan tradition. Moon Books invites you to begin or to deepen your own encounter, right here, right now. If you have enjoyed this book, why not tell other readers by posting a review on your preferred book site.

Recent bestsellers from Moon Books are:

Journey to the Dark Goddess
How to Return to Your Soul
Jane Meredith
Discover the powerful secrets of the Dark Goddess and
transform your depression, grief and pain into healing
and integration.
Paperback: 978-1-84694-677-6 ebook: 978-1-78099-223-5

Shamanic Reiki
Expanded Ways of Working with Universal Life Force Energy
Llyn Roberts, Robert Levy
Shamanism and Reiki are each powerful ways of healing; together,
their power multiplies. *Shamanic Reiki* introduces techniques to
help healers and Reiki practitioners tap ancient healing wisdom.
Paperback: 978-1-84694-037-8 ebook: 978-1-84694-650-9

Pagan Portals – The Awen Alone
Walking the Path of the Solitary Druid
Joanna van der Hoeven
An introductory guide for the solitary Druid, *The Awen Alone* will
accompany you as you explore, and seek out your own place
within the natural world.
Paperback: 978-1-78279-547-6 ebook: 978-1-78279-546-9

A Kitchen Witch's World of Magical Herbs & Plants
Rachel Patterson
A journey into the magical world of herbs and plants, filled with
magical uses, folklore, history and practical magic. By popular
writer, blogger and kitchen witch, Tansy Firedragon.
Paperback: 978-1-78279-621-3 ebook: 978-1-78279-620-6

Medicine for the Soul
The Complete Book of Shamanic Healing
Ross Heaven
All you will ever need to know about shamanic healing and how to
become your own shaman…
Paperback: 978-1-78099-419-2 ebook: 978-1-78099-420-8

Shaman Pathways – The Druid Shaman
Exploring the Celtic Otherworld
Danu Forest
A practical guide to Celtic shamanism with exercises and
techniques as well as traditional lore for exploring the Celtic
Otherworld.
Paperback: 978-1-78099-615-8 ebook: 978-1-78099-616-5

Traditional Witchcraft for the Woods and Forests
A Witch's Guide to the Woodland with Guided Meditations and
Pathworking
Mélusine Draco
A Witch's guide to walking alone in the woods, with guided
meditations and pathworking.
Paperback: 978-1-84694-803-9 ebook: 978-1-84694-804-6

Naming the Goddess
Trevor Greenfield
Naming the Goddess is written by over eighty adherents and
scholars of Goddess and Goddess Spirituality.
Paperback: 978-1-78279-476-9 ebook: 978-1-78279-475-2

Shapeshifting into Higher Consciousness
Heal and Transform Yourself and Our World with Ancient
Shamanic and Modern Methods
Llyn Roberts
Ancient and modern methods that you can use every day to
transform yourself and make a positive difference in the world.
Paperback: 978-1-84694-843-5 ebook: 978-1-84694-844-2

Readers of ebooks can buy or view any of these bestsellers by
clicking on the live link in the title. Most titles are published in
paperback and as an ebook. Paperbacks are available in traditional
bookshops. Both print and ebook formats are available online.

Find more titles and sign up to our readers' newsletter at
http://www.johnhuntpublishing.com/paganism
Follow us on Facebook at https://www.facebook.com/MoonBooks
and Twitter at https://twitter.com/MoonBooksJHP